# Escort girl

**Melodie Nelson**

# Escort girl

## A Personal Memoir

Published by Transit Publishing Inc.

ISBN: 978-1-926745-49-7

Cover design: François Turgeon
Text design and composition: Nassim Bahloul


Cover photo: © Joseph Elfassi
Author photos: © BTH

Transit Publishing Inc.
279 Sherbrooke West
Montreal, QC
Canada
H2X 1Y2

Tel: 514-273-0123
www.transitpublishing.com

Printed and Bound in Italy

# Table of Contents

# No to Hypocrisy, Long Live Sex and Godiva Chocolates

I'm eighteen, there's no dildo in my bedside table, and I marry the first guy I ever kissed. We went to the same private high school in an eastern suburb of Montreal. When we were fifteen, he asked me over the phone to be his girlfriend, then dumped me two weeks later because he wanted more time to play baseball and smoke joints with his friends. I slept with ten guys and some years later we find each other again and fall in love because we both adore Portishead and David Cronenberg.

A year after our wedding, we're living in an apartment, and I have a hard time juggling being a full-time literature student, a part-time library clerk, and a spoiled brat who gets bored easily and who wants a new life every first of the month. So I quit my job and answer a want ad in a local paper looking for sexy waitresses.

I'm now waitressing at a very shady restaurant called Les Princesses d'Hochelaga in Montreal. Most of my conversations with other waitresses revolve around *Occupation Double*, a Quebecois version of *Big Brother*, and other reality TV shows. I eat too much bacon and pose as a French immigrant because I don't like using Quebec expressions, and I sit on the lap of truckers with black teeth. I stop working early in the fall because standing from 5 A.M. to 2 P.M. in an underheated restaurant with the door continually opening and closing, wearing only sandals and a short skirt, makes me sick. I take this opportunity to get two kittens, the very ugly but cuddly Syphilis and Porcelaine, along with a DVD player, a jelly dildo, Geisha balls, and lots of chocolate bars from the Belgian chocolate-maker Godiva.

I start doing sexy webcam shows in front of three computer screens, I insert my fingers or sex toys into my pussy, I make small talk with men, I write horoscopes for a cultural magazine in Montreal, and sometimes I even do my homework in front of the cameras. I attend literature classes at the University of Quebec in Montreal where I draw women on all fours in my notebooks and my husband is in my classes. He brings home pizza from the restaurant where he cooks and comforts me when I cry while reading *The Sisterhood of the Traveling Pants*. He's such a nice guy, though he only gets a hard-on once a week. I cheat on him without remorse, giving a friend a blow job in Le Petit Moulinsart restaurant and fucking another friend at the trendy Belgo art gallery.

Staring at three computer screens for six consecutive hours three nights a week gives me repeated conjunctivitis, forcing me to wear unsexy glasses. Dancing in front of unknown peeping Toms soon bores me so I stop my webcam broadcasts. I pose for *Hustler* in my half-basement apartment, which makes me ecstatic, and I get a check for $500 signed by Larry Flynt. I photocopy the check as a keepsake, I cash it wearing a schoolgirl uniform, and I allow myself another month to procrastinate about finding a serious job. I then do sexy phone calls with a steamy French accent for the ridiculous rate of 25 cents per minute. Afterwards I become a bookseller for Archambault, where I gaze at Japanese manga full of girls with big boobs getting raped by the ice cream man, and books about perverts getting aroused by women dressed up as insects. I need to work more than thirty hours a week to get by, which I don't. Instead I keep on buying Old Navy shirts and that really gets me down. Putting the latest Marc Levy book on display in the window of the bookstore and attending university classes where we discuss the meaning of trees in modern Quebec literature wear me out. I count every penny to be able to afford subway tickets, I think about seeing a doctor to get a Xanax prescription, and I drink too many sugar-free Red Bulls.

One day, *La Presse* newspaper publishes a story about escorts who claim to like their job and have never been threatened by their clients. I find these girls glamorous. They make me want to stop fucking for free, and forget about all those guys who rejected me in high school and college when I was fifteen, sixteen, seventeen with my black fuck-me boots while I walked and talked too loudly, and guys on the street asked me if I were a hooker. I wasn't happy, far from it, I only existed when I was desired and any rejection meant I was worthless. All my friends had said *no* to me at least once. They thought I was only hurting myself by trying to find myself in other people's arms and not wearing any underwear under my Goth dresses. Being an escort would allow me to earn a living from this desire of mine, and no one would ever reject me again. I thought being married to a nice and loving guy would be enough but I find that life to be an utter bore.

I meet an escort, a friend of a cousin of mine, and she persuades me to join an agency. I become an escort, just like that, because I want to see the most luxurious hotel rooms in Montreal, to be independent, so I don't owe my parents or my husband for those seven hundred pairs of shoes in my closet or for my leisure days, far from my university classes. My days spent applying Chanel nail polish while reading celebrity gossip are making my daily life much more interesting than all the other literature students who smoke joints, talk about Quebec's independence, and only shave once a month. I become an escort mainly because I love to fuck, but also to say goodbye to bosses criticizing me for taking sixteen-minute breaks instead of fifteen-minute ones.

I become an escort so I can have a white Louis Vuitton handbag with little cherries on it, like the one actress and *Playboy* model Carmen Electra has in the latest *Us Weekly* magazine, because I've always had the impression whores know so much more than other girls about men and life in general, because I want to feel pretty, and because I think working in high heels is much more fun than wearing flats.

Four years have passed and I am no longer an escort, but I loved the experience, which is far less dangerous than giving your phone number to strangers you meet in bars or at the bus stop. I worked as a professional call girl going from houses to hotel rooms, with a chauffeur as well as an in-call escort in a downtown Montreal apartment rented by the lady in charge of the escort agency. She gave a little extra to the building owner to make sure there wouldn't be any trouble with the police, because although prostitution is tolerated in Quebec, hypocritically the act of making money satisfying clients' needs isn't. Being an escort made me a calm and open-minded person, comfortable with my femininity and my desires, and allowed me to meet interesting men to whom I brought happiness for thirty or sixty minutes. I met a lot of proud girls, who never shed tears between clients, fun and cultured girls wearing designer shades, who took hairdressing classes and shared a slice of all-dressed pizza with their girlfriends. Girls like me, who didn't get raped by their grandfather on Christmas Eve under the watchful eye of a moose head adorning the wall, and who never, despite popular belief, had to suck dad's cock after he had fucked the baby sitter.

After the first year and a half, I couldn't imagine getting

up on a Friday morning and doing anything other than spending the day in bed, being someone's fantasy, therapist, or fake girlfriend, for extremely charming clients. It all seemed so easy, except when my body tired or hurt from being penetrated so often, and I had to lie to my girlfriends and my family by making up stories about an imaginary job. In a way, I was hiding.

What I found the hardest was to think of lies to tell others. But now I no longer want to be quiet. I want to take responsibility for my actions and not feel insulted by the word *whore*. I want to show that being an escort means taking advantage of my own pleasure and body, and offering it this way is nicer and easier than setting up books in a store display or serving pitchers of beer in a bar several nights a week. If Paris Hilton and Kim Kardashian can do porn films and become mainstream stars, if girls can wear T-shirts with *Open 24/7* on them and brag about frenching their girlfriends in cabs, if *Cosmopolitan* can run stories like *All New 50 Sex Tricks* or *Sex He Craves* or *The Easy Way to Boost Your Sex Drive*, if men can buy packs of beer in the hope of getting their pictures taken their faces deep in the cleavage of some girl dressed up as a maid at the Coors Light Mansion, can we start accepting that prostitutes love their job and stop denigrating them by viewing them as victims?

I chose to be an escort. And it was the best decision of my life.

# A Future Bimbo Addicted to Lubricant?

One October evening, while drinking quart after quart of green tea with my cousin, she lets me know about her friend Nathalie, who's been an escort for a couple of months and enjoys it very much. She goes to the luxurious Ritz Hotel, works three nights a week, and spends the rest of her time knitting and doing taxidermy. Knowing that every escort is not a bimbo addicted to martinis, blow, and Juicy Couture clothes like those worn by Eva Longoria makes me cheerful. My cousin gives me Nathalie's phone number so I can ask her a million questions; she knows that, since I was sixteen, I believed I was destined to become a whore. I'm not quite sure why. Some people smoke weed, drink too much, buy lottery tickets, or watch the reality show *Occupation Double* each night. I fuck to cure my boredom and to forget I'll never be pretty enough to become Miss Canada. I think getting paid to spread my legs, getting paid to apply makeup, getting paid to wear five-inch-heel boots, getting paid to say things like, "Do you want me to lick your balls?" is amazing!

I call Nathalie, who tells me she loves coming back home to her gay roommates after fucking four or five guys and spilling the beans. She can talk for hours, while smoking a cigarette, about this guy's hairy back or that guy's probing tongue. She laughs and tells me it's not dangerous, she never met a single girl threatened by a client, and only knows of one girl who does coke before going to work. I ask her how I should dress if I ever decide to get into her line of work and she insists, "No jeans, it's not classy enough. I always dress in black." I then ask her for her agency's phone number and she wishes me luck for the conversation I'll eventually have with my boyfriend.

From the start, Samuel refuses, "I don't want you making love to strangers."

I ask him stupidly, "Even if I close my eyes?"

He looks so sad when he answers, "Yes, even if you close your eyes and think of me while fucking your clients." He pictures me in the local news section of the newspaper *La Presse*, "Dead at 19, murdered by a man who bashed her head against a brick wall before raping her."

I tell him about Nathalie and her experiences, about clients becoming regulars, I assure him Nathalie's not undergoing therapy and she doesn't need sleeping pills, anxiolytics, or drugs to make her life more bearable, that she only fucks for $200 a pop, and incidentally embalms dead animals. I tell him I only want to try, just this one time, and then I'll either resume living my depressing life of being both a student and bookseller, or start wearing thigh-highs three nights a week. He accepts, he always bears with my whims, and lights a cigarette as he starts doing dishes, staring out the window of our basement apartment onto our cul-de-sac.

I hate him for willingly sharing me with other men, just because I asked him to. I sometimes hate everybody. At the bookstore, I hate my colleagues for saying I'm not eating enough when they see me have half a vegetable soup for lunch, I hate my boss who at closing always checks to see if I've stolen any CDs by forcing me to open my purse and show her my tampons and American women's magazines, thus making me miss the bus, I hate the books I have to sell, I hate Nelly Arcan because every couple buying *Folle* or *Whore* seems to want to do a threesome with me. I hate my parents for telling me to keep studying and not go to Australia for six months to photograph koalas, and I hate the winter and my not-warm-enough coat. I think I could learn not to hate everything if all I had to do was smile, hold out my hand to receive bills, and get down on all fours on a hotel room bed.

When Samuel leaves to go work at an Italian restaurant on Sherbrooke Street East, fifteen minutes from our apartment, I call the agency. A woman answers, I declare my intentions of working for her, she asks my age, measurements, and length of hair, and how well I can speak English. She offers to start me that very night and I accept. I tell her I want to be called Marissa. I just watched the whole first season of *The O.C.* Marissa Cooper's character, played by Mischa Barton, is my favorite. I see myself in this pretty young woman, a little too skinny, from a well-to-do family, but lost, without ties, who pretends she's having fun sipping fruity drinks in a bikini by the pool. The lady from the agency tells me a driver will come pick me up around 8:30.

I spread my skirts and stockings on my bed. My head still full of stereotypes, I believe every escort should wear them. I choose a black miniskirt and a black camisole with embroidered white flowers around the neck. I ruin a pair of thigh-high stockings by trying to put them on too fast and a second pair by running into my boyfriend's guitar. I am stressed out, I feel like crying, I want to cancel my evening plans and go shop for new toys for my kittens. I finally take my *Magic 8-ball,* a pool hall version of the fortune cookie telling you your future, and ask it out loud if my evening will go well. I flip it over and read, *Absolutely.*

Before the driver picks me up, I have time to drink two sugar-free Red Bulls, wonder a thousand times if the clients will like my breasts smaller than Kate Moss' or Paris Hilton's, and reapply lip plumper about twenty thousand times. I leave a note for my boyfriend on the living-room table, covered in fashion magazines and shag, and follow the driver to his rusty car. I don't know if I should sit next to him, or in the back seat, so I choose to sit in front and tell him it's my first time. He says it's also his, he had volunteered his services a month ago but was only called now. He's cute, he looks like a guy from the suburbs of Montreal, his hair full of gel and sporting a fake tan. While driving to a Longueuil hotel to fuck my first client, who regularly trains new escorts, the driver tells me about his eighteen-year-old girlfriend. She's very open minded and would like to do threesomes with a girl as pretty as me. I smile and decline, demoralized. By deciding to become a whore, I've chosen to stop giving it away for free and to focus only on what my pussy can bring me. The driver apologizes and keeps on talking about the dirty Website he visits. Uneasy, he asks me to call him as soon as I'm done with the client, an hour later, otherwise he'll come get me with a knife hidden in his leather-coat pocket. Though I think he's exaggerating a bit, I find him sweet for worrying about me like this.

In the hotel bar, Marie-Chantal Toupin sings songs from her latest album and I pass several men who don't even give me a second look, even though my so-called stay-ups roll down every five steps. I find my first client's room after double checking the room number with the agency. I knock, a nervous smile on my face, and quickly spit my mint-flavored gum into a tissue. A man, about forty-five or fifty years old, wearing dark jeans, opens the door and kisses my cheeks. He has a pleasant aftershave smell. He offers me a glass of water and seems happy I know Nathalie. He asks me to lie down on the bed. He undresses, turns on the radio, looks for a French-language station, and lies down next to me. He kisses my neck, brings my camisole up to gently suck my nipples while I look at us in the ceiling mirror. I find myself pretty, my long black hair reaching the middle of my back, my eyes painted with burgundy eye shadow, and my breasts pointing upwards. I think I'm prettier than with my Archambault uniform vest, or my trendy student skinny jeans.

He takes off my underwear with his teeth, coats his dick with lubricant before putting a condom on and lubricating it. I find it strange and ask him why he has to lubricate so much. He penetrates me with two fingers and then wipes his wet fingers on my skirt, before pushing his dick into my pussy. I don't know how to touch him. I put my legs around his back and look at him on top of me, until he comes, his eyes shut tight. He gets up, one hand crushing his limp penis and goes to take a shower, I stay on the bed, trying out various fake orgasm faces in the mirror. I'm relieved, being a whore seems easy, and I wonder if all the clients will be like him.

Before returning to my driver, my first client asks me what my schedule will be like with the agency and tells me about his condo in Hochelaga-Maisonneuve, a working-class Montreal neighborhood, twenty minutes from downtown, where the construction of pricy modern condos infuriates longstanding residents. My client loses his temper about the rules of his condominium banning all bird-feeders, and tells me how he circumvents that by putting blue jay bird-feed directly on his balcony floor. I find his love for critters touching, but so fucking boring!

I give $20 to my driver and $80 to the agency and we're off to get another escort. The super classy and gorgeous Moroccan girl named Isabelle says hello to me before begging the driver to go buy her some condoms in a nearby drugstore open till midnight, telling him she's too shy and that he can keep the change. While she does a client in a downtown hotel, the driver takes me to Ville Saint Laurent to meet a young and sexy client who downs two shots of whisky and fucks me with a neon yellow cock-ring around his dick.

Around 1 A.M., the driver tells us heating the car requires too much gas and offers to stop in a McDonald's. He orders a chicken nugget combo and the other escort eats her fries with mayonnaise. I refuse to order anything, I don't want to look like I'm two months pregnant for the next clients or smell like ketchup. Isabelle asks me if I have a boyfriend. She thinks I'm lucky that I didn't have to lie to Samuel, she dates a guy whose professional contract in New York City ends in three months, and who comes to see her in Montreal every weekend. She says one of her friends works on cruise ships and she plans on doing the same, maybe next summer or the summer after that or in two years, after finishing her psychology studies at the University of Montreal.

The driver gets an urgent call, he says we have to go near Villa-Maria metro station, in a multiethnic neighborhood of Montreal where Polish bakeries and Mediterranean restaurants adjoin yoga centers and designer children's wear stores. I discover Montreal by night and find it beautiful, I've been here almost a year and all I know of the city are secondhand booksellers and Mont Royal Street thrift stores. Isabelle goes to see the client while the driver and I wait for her, humming Beyoncé's *Naughty Girl*. She comes back an hour later and tells me, "He wants you now. He couldn't fuck me, he's coked out of his mind."

The guy had left his spacious apartment door wide open, I close it behind me, he gets up, pays me while telling me he likes my skirt. He offers me a line of coke, I politely decline, and he does one using a rolled-up $20 bill as a straw. I start caressing his cock, it's limp, I get down on my knees, my mouth full with his balls, my hands on his ass. He says, "Later, we're in no hurry, right?" We sit on the couch and watch infomercials for an hour. I leave him with the urge to buy a Magic Bullet blender as soon as possible.

I finally come home around 7 A.M., my boyfriend is up, ready to leave the apartment to get to his first class of the day. I am tired but very proud of myself, my services are no longer free, I even get paid to put my finger in asses. Samuel offers me a strawberry breakfast Pop-Tart. I show him all my twenty- and fifty-dollar bills and I hide the money between the pages of a Pedro Juan Gutierrez book. I kiss my boyfriend for ten minutes straight without taking time to catch my breath and tell him many times that we need to buy a Magic Bullet, I then eat Alpha-Bits cereal, and fall asleep in front of an episode of *The Simple Life.*

I decide to quit Archambault in no time and I let a blondie with glasses who'll surely turn into a vicious advertising director fuck me standing against the wall of the employees' bathroom. Two days later, right after a creative writing class where I fought with a greasy-haired girl about my abundant use of the word *pussy* in my text, the lady from the escort agency calls me. She asks me if I can be ready in thirty minutes, there's someone in a Laval hotel room who wants to ass-fuck me. I say yes, I have lots of watermelon and Pina Colada-flavored condoms in my purse and I'm wearing a dark blue negligee under my long black vest.

It'll be my first anal sex experience, I am stressed out and excited, I'm going to get an extra $100 tonight. I hope I'm not going to stain the sheets. I also hope the guy's dick is abnormally short.

I knock at Room 216 and hear a woman's voice, I realize the girl from the agency gave me the wrong room number and I want to kill her. I call her, feeling humiliated in my fuck-me boots, alone in a corridor. She apologizes and directs me to the man who's going to fuck my anus for the very first time. He's watching porn on a giant TV screen, a discolored

23

girl licks another fake blonde girl's hole. He gives me $350, which I don't count right away. I put the money in my purse, pretending not to care about being here just to show him my pear-shaped ass. I open the client's white bathrobe and start fellating him. He had washed his dick and the soap numbs my mouth. He throws me on the bed, my head turned to watch the porn film. I want the two bleached girls with breasts as round as soccer balls to be my only concern as his saliva drips between my ass cheeks. He penetrates my pussy for a few seconds, to ease my mind, but I'm gripping the bed sheets too tightly with my nails hastily done the night before. When he slides half his cock in my ass, I scream, he stops moving, and I say, "Sorry, continue, continue," and he puts the rest in, holding me flat on the bed. I can't raise my head. I clench my jaw and count the seconds, I think about the winter boot selection at Browns and which ones I'll take after my tremendous anal pain.

I feel like leaving, he ejaculates, and we stay there watching the porn film for a few moments before he asks me to ride him. I don't know if I have to ask him for extra money for a second fuck or if I can say no. But time passes and he can't reach a second orgasm, I leave without showering, forgetting my purse in his hotel room. I come back ten minutes later and my client's reading the business newspaper *Les Affaires* while eating a watermelon. He opens my mouth and makes me eat a few juicy chunks. I ask the driver to bring me home right away because I don't think I can keep on working. My legs are shaking, I feel sick for having wanted his dick up my ass, I want to close my eyes and erase that evening from my mind, and not see all the Christmas lights hanging from all the houses. I don't want to think about Christmas, or my parents who'll unwrap my presents not knowing I paid for them with lubricant dripping from my ass.

In the following week, the agency offers me that same

Laval client, but I decline, never wanting to be sodomized again by anything bigger than a one-inch-long cock. I see my first client quite often, two or three times a week, without going through the agency. He picks me up at home and we always go back to the same hotel room with the mirror on the ceiling. He fucks me, each time putting a whole bottle of lubricant on his dick. Afterwards he tells me about his health problems, he has ringing in his ears, and discusses his hobbies. He loves photography, he bought loads of expensive equipment that's now sitting in the closet next to a tennis racquet, diving gear, and paint brushes bought at the artist supplies store Omer DeSerres. He loses interest very rapidly. He now wants to learn how to play didgeridoo and hopes I'll never have my period.

One night, I'm drinking a Smirnoff Ice in a bar with some former Archambault colleagues, a girl with platinum blond and black hair, not unlike a skunk, and a guy who looks like a Viking. My cell phone keeps ringing. I'm late to meet a client, but I don't feel like starting my night right away. I want to keep on laughing and talking about *Gilmore Girls* with them, but I take the call in the bar's bathroom and I say that I'll be ready in fifteen minutes. I leave my former colleagues, almost ready to tell them I'm leaving to get fucked at the Delta Hotel. I want to tell them, I want to laugh and bet with them that the guy screwing me will have a cock the size of a can of cola, but I keep my mouth shut. I don't want them holding me back, telling me I don't have to collect condoms in my purse and dicks in my pussy.

At the Delta, I walk past the reception desk like I'm one of their guests, and with my vintage coat too big for me and my hair full of snow I simply don't look like an escort. When I get to the room, two Asian businessmen are waiting for me with Bianca, a gorgeous Latina whose breasts are as big as Victoria Beckham's. I drop my coat on the floor and take off my white shirt and red, yellow, and navy-blue plaid schoolgirl skirt. Bianca's in bed with one Asian man who's fucking her underneath the covers. My client asks me to lie on my side and not move while he fucks me for three minutes tops while I try to see Bianca's breasts. When Bianca and I start getting dressed, my client says he's not sure Bianca's breasts are fake, Bianca protests, and he pays her $20 to touch them. Bianca's milk chocolate-colored boobs seem flabby. I wish men would pay me to suck them for thirty minutes.

In the lobby of the Delta, Bianca and I wait for our drivers, mine arrives first, and I bid her good night. She nods. In the car, a thirty-something blonde with fake nails like those of the black American marathon runners in the Olympic Games shows me pictures of her two kids. She asks the driver to stop at a Tim Hortons for a cup of coffee. She just spent two hours with a couple and says, "I like licking pussy, but when it takes too long, I just want to slap her and say go to a new hairdresser, fuck, that girl I just did had the same hairdo I had in my high school graduation photos, and that was fifteen years ago, goddammit!" The driver goes into the coffee shop with her and stays in the bathroom a long time, which worries the blonde girl once she gets back into the car. She's sure he's doing drugs and calls the agency to complain.

When we get going towards Montreal's East End, the driver starts driving erratically on the highway, changing lanes too quickly, going against traffic, about ready to hit another car or a bridge pillar. I'm sure I'm about to die and the fact that even though I'm closing my eyes I can't see my life flashing before me is frustrating. I want to see myself as a ballerina dancing in front of the tender eyes of my grandmother, I want to see my ten-year-old self winning the gold medal in a ski competition, I want to see myself throwing snowballs at my brothers, I want to see myself reaching orgasm for the first time with Olivier while watching *A Clockwork Orange*, I want to see myself french-kissing my best friend, I want to see myself dancing on Spice Girls songs, I want to see myself sucking my drama teacher's cock in his office, I want to see my mother holding me in her arms, and my father doing the same, I want to smell my first dog and feel nothing when the driver collides head on with another car or pillar. He finally manages to get control of the car and I can still hear the other escort yelling at him, shouting that he's an asshole and forcing him to bring us both home.

As soon as I get home, I ask my boyfriend to make me a cheeseburger and I cry without telling him why. I empty my purse and give him half my bills, and decide to stop working for an out-call agency. I spend all I have on Christmas presents for my family and my kittens, Syphilis and Porcelaine. I buy a long low-cut black dress I wear to midnight mass and I stare at myself in the bathroom mirror for a long time at my parents' cottage, wondering if one day a client will stain it with his cum.

After having a month-long period because I take the pill continuously so I won't have to stop seeing clients, I look through the weekly *Hour* newspaper to find escort agencies or little old men wanting to receive wet underwear by mail. I dial a random number after reading an article about a seventy-year-old Italian woman who had given birth and when a woman answers, I tell her I have experience and want to work for her as an in-call escort. She asks me how much I weigh, and I reply, " My weight is 105 lb, my bra size is 32A, and I have a 23-inch waist." She says she had several girls who claimed they were skinny but ended up being thirty pounds heavier. I assure her that when I step on the scale in high heels and a wet T-shirt, it shows 105 lb. She asks me how old I am. I say, "nineteen," and she replies, "We'll say you're 18 on our Website." She asks me to meet her that afternoon and see the apartment.

I'm really hoping the lady from the agency will find me adorable because being an in-call escort would allow me to entertain clients in a fixed location without having to go all over Montreal with a driver, freezing my tits in an unheated car. Between clients, I could study, do yoga, and call my mom. I can't wait to see the apartments. I'm not sure what to expect, a crazy dungeon or a high-class loft with a canopy bed and a huge Jacuzzi.

I get to Durocher Street in my jeans and baby blue

sweater, near Place-des-Arts metro station and designer boutiques such as Estrada and Dior. I'm anxious to meet the agency's owner. I redo my hair in the elevator. Debbie, the agency's madam, greets me in a two-bedroom apartment on the fourth floor. Her dirty blonde hair showing an inch of gray roots, she looks at me and says I'm pretty; she'll introduce me as the escort who looks like a model. I think that would be right if models were five-foot-four, wore less makeup than fourteen-year-old teenagers, and had a big Jewish nose. She asks me if I have a change of clothes. I say yes. I had anticipated she might want to take pictures of me, which isn't the case, she just wants me to start that very evening. She adds that it's okay if I don't have condoms with me, there's a convenience store just across the street.

I hesitate for a few seconds, wondering if I have time to tell Samuel and if I have enough energy to fuck nonstop till midnight. In any case, I agree to start in an hour. Debbie, seems happy and shows me where she keeps the bed sheets and towels. She specifies I shouldn't offer a new towel to each client who wants to shower. "I don't have time to do loads all day, so let one dry on the heater when you're with a client and then put it back in the closet." I try not to look shocked. I couldn't imagine offering the same towel to two clients. She shows me the list of rules posted on a wall. All escorts must call twenty-four hours in advance if they're not coming in or they'll be fined $50. We have to empty the trash cans and change the bed sheets after every shift. Doing drugs means getting fired, and the TV must be on all the time so neighbors won't hear us screaming. Jeans are forbidden, we must be on time or get penalized for each missed block of fifteen minutes, we have to sweep the floor of the entrance to remove all the pebbles left by our clients' boots, we have to put half of what our clients give us in a white envelope locked in a safety deposit box on the kitchen counter, hidden underneath a fake rose in a vase and some fabric. The penalties kind of irritate me, I understand tardiness is bad for the agency's image, but no other type of job would dare ask this of its employees. I decide not to complain. At least the lady from the agency won't be like my boss at Archambault, continually following me around checking to see if I might be the next employee of the month, always polite and willing to help clients.

She leaves me alone in the apartment, telling me she usually answers the phone. Exceptionally tonight, she's going out, and a friend of hers, who used to own a sex-toy shop, will be the male receptionist. She also lets me know her son lives in the apartment across the hallway and he'll be the one collecting money at the end of the night. If there's any problem, I have to contact him before thinking of calling the cops. He won't think twice about beating up a bad client. She guesses this makes me nervous and adds, "Our clients are nice, but you never know, especially at night, some drink a little too much. If they offer you some alcohol, you can have one beer, but brush your teeth afterwards. I don't want the next clients thinking you're a problem girl."

I call my boyfriend and let him know I won't be coming home until 1 A.M. I tell him the apartment's perfectly nice, the walls have been recently painted an eggshell color, there's Asian artwork in every room, my boss talks about her dog as much as she does about clients, I have a room of my own, a private lounge with a TV, and all the latest Disney films. He says to call him whenever I feel like it and wishes me luck. I hang up, looking at my cell phone with eyes as sad as a stuffed puppy's. Just for a moment. I would have liked spending the evening with him, asking him what nail polish color would be the prettiest on my toenails, eating butter-free popcorn, and listening for the hundredth time this week to Martha Wainwright's album.

I get changed in front of an old episode of *The Simple Life*: Paris and Nicole are working in a funeral home and spill some guy's ashes on the carpet. I let my Garage-brand jeans lie around on the couch, I stretch wearing a black mini and black and white polka-dot vintage high heels, waiting for the first client. The phone rings and it's Raymond, the former sex-toy shop owner. "Your first client will be here in ten minutes, gorgeous. His name's Bernard, just like former Quebec premier Bernard Landry. I live in Verchères, just across from Bernard Landry, and I tell him to fuck off every time I see him. I have to hold back from vandalizing his car, but I write him anonymous letters. Fucking separatist."

I'm sitting on the kitchen counter, waiting for my first client, my legs dangling, my eyes fixed on the door. He knocks. I look through the peephole. He has dark hair and a fleshy mouth, just like the first guy who made me come. I open the door and before he has time to take off his coat, I smile, put my hands on his shoulders, stand on tiptoe, and kiss him on the mouth. He tosses me against the fridge and raises one of my legs. I can feel his cock erect against my coral-colored underwear. This excites me. I think of Samuel, how he never takes me like this in our kitchen. Hanging his coat on the coat-rack, Bernard says, "You can call your boss and tell him I'll stay an hour instead of a half-hour." He washes his hands after paying me, and I wait for him in the bedroom. I'm wondering if I should get undressed or wait for him. I take off my shoes and sit on the bed, looking at my toes, thinking I'll never get foot fetishists who want perfect feet because my feet are those of a girl who's been wearing shoes a bit too tight for the last decade. I put my shoes back on and tilt my head to the side so he'll think of me as a collectible porcelain doll. He comes in and stands between my legs, pushing my underwear aside, and slides a finger into my pussy. He kisses my clit and I gently stop him, saying, "I love getting licked, but you have to pay extra for that." I'm feeling embarrassed, talking about extras. I hate talking about money. I wish clients could forget I get paid for all they do to me.

He lies down on the bed and I straddle him, kissing him, while stroking his chest with my hard nipples. I keep my eyes open, his are glittering. I go down between his legs and start licking his balls. I fumble to find a condom and ask him to put it on because I can't, fearing I'd rip it with my fake nails. I don't have any lubricant with me and that annoys me because I won't be able to do many clients before I'll feel like I have a sandpaper vagina. He tells me he wants me doggy-style and fucks me so hard the bed on wheels knocks against the wall. I can't help giggling, nervously, thinking about the sounds the other tenants below me can hear. Fortunately, the bedroom's next to a stairwell no one uses, not another apartment, otherwise I wouldn't be able to touch another dick without fearing someone calling the vice squad.

When Bernard leaves, I tell Raymond I'm once more alone, wet, smiling, and not sporting a shiner. I open all the cupboards, steal Ringolos from a bag started by another escort, leaf through one *Loulou*, one *Star Inc.*, and one *InStyle*. Dita Von Teese shopping at Whole Foods Market in an emerald green dress makes me want to touch myself.

I get another call. I look at my reflection in the bathroom mirror, reapply concealer and eye shadow, and welcome a forty-something guy in a gray shirt and dark suit panto. He wants to sit in the living room, not go straight to the bedroom. The agency's owner told me the living room is the escorts' private space, where girls can leave ashtrays and open notebooks covered in class notes, so I refuse. He says he only wants to talk, so I'll feel less like he's objectifying me than if we went to the bedroom. He seems nice, so I accept.

He tells me he just had a five-course dinner at Europea. He wants to continue having a pleasant evening with me before going to see *2046*, the new Wong Kar-Wai film. I envy him. I'm dying to see this movie myself. We talk about foreign films and their traditions, and Tatin pie. I'm afraid the client will think I'm on coke because I can't stop giggling, like a girl from a private school talking to her first crush.

While we're chatting, he's sliding down my skirt and caressing my thighs. I sit on his lap. He asks me to get up, bend over, and touch the ground so he can see my ass. Obeying him turns me on. I stand before him, stepping in front of the TV airing home decorating shows, and I feel his tongue slide between my asshole and pussy. He makes me come while I talk about the class I took on Duras, Angot, and Ernaux. Then I go down on him, without a condom, and he ejaculates on the sofa. I'm not wiping it off. I don't give a fuck about stains.

I call Samuel, tell him I never thought clients could get me so wet, tell him I love him a thousand times, and he tells me I should hop in a cab when I'm done so I can be in his arms as soon as possible. I tell him I might stop at the grocery store to get a can of seafood for the kittens. I also tell him I want to move; living on a cul-de-sac next to a McDonald's open 24/7, and only seeing fat girls on the sidewalks by Langelier metro station is really getting me down. I want to live elsewhere, closer to my favorite shops, organic produce stores, and French bakeries. He agrees and says he'll look in the classifieds the next day for apartments for rent on the Plateau and adds he'd also like a new guitar.

I write it down in a Paperblanks notebook where I write all our desires and their costs, from a flat-screen TV to mini-skis, to a white Louis Vuitton handbag with cherries on it like Carmen Electra's. I used to be hopeless in arithmetic when I was studying in a private school but now, in my coral underwear, in a furnished two-bedroom apartment without a calculator, I'm amazing. It takes me two seconds to know how many blow-jobs with a condom I have to do to pay for a month's groceries, and how many blow jobs without a condom I have to do to afford a new pair of flat shoes, and how many facials I must receive to buy a thirty-piece sushi platter at Zenya.

I tear the page with Dita Von Teese from the magazine and put it in my notebook. A client arrives, a carrot-top with curly hair. He makes me think of a buck hunter with his plaid shirt and his belly sticking out of his tight jeans. He kisses my cheeks, I unbutton his shirt, fighting with the buttons. He asks me if I have a boyfriend and I lie, "No, guys don't like me, I swear I'll end up living alone with five or six cats, llamas, and chickens on a farm." I believe every escort should say she's single, to give the impression she could be a future girlfriend, or is too kinky to want to sleep next to the same man each night.

The carrot-top's wife has just left him, he doesn't know why, he puts me on top of him, my knees on the sheets, his hands on my waist. He wants to know my age. I say, "What did they tell you on the phone? Eighteen? Do you think I look older or younger?" He comes quickly, holding onto the condom when I move to lie down next to him. I show him the trash can, underneath a mahogany writing desk. He throws the condom in, puts his gray underwear on and joins me in bed. I play with his curly chest hair. I get another call. I apologize to the client and take a quick shower, trying to keep my hair from getting wet.

I call Raymond and tell him I cannot take any more clients after this one because I ran out of condoms and the convenience store must be closed by now. I'm surprised at how easy it is being an in-call escort. On my first evening, I got more clients than I did as an out-call escort and I can fantasize about Paris Hilton and her Chihuahua without fearing a client might steal my money while I'm in his shower. A guy almost seven feet tall knocks at the door. His head is shaved and he looks like Mickey Rourke before his face got all deformed from too many plastic surgeries and boxing matches.

The way he slowly undresses me turns me on. He caresses me and I love his big, hard hands. I'd like to offer him some of my Aveeno lotion. He offers me $30 to lick my pussy and I answer with a smile, he spreads my legs, spits on my clit, and does slow circles. I stiffen. He nibbles the inside of my thighs and I can feel his tongue move between my lips. I hope I don't taste too much like latex. I think about Samuel, maybe I'll give him a blow job later, before going to sleep, maybe he's playing with himself while taking a bubble bath, looking at big-titted girls in *Cheri* or *Penthouse*, or maybe he's smoking too many cigarettes, worrying about me. Maybe I should give him a trip to Cuba in exchange for his quitting smoking. I look at one of Mickey Rourke's tattoos, a yin-yang symbol on his forearm. I can't come, I invite him to penetrate me with his dick, "I want you, I want to please you, I can't stay like this any longer with your head between my legs." He comes on top of me, caressing my breasts, taking his time with each one. He kisses them and sucks on them, "You have beautiful breasts, promise me you'll never get a breast augmentation." He's not the first client to tell me this and I love it, I need to hear a thousand times a day that I'm pretty, I wouldn't have made it as a bookseller with glasses without wanting to burst into tears in my turtlenecks. I thought I wouldn't be as popular with my 32A bras, but my clients love the fact I'm as nature made me, with my mini-boobs always rock-hard, my somewhat messy hair, and my subtle use of makeup.

Mickey Rourke comes while looking at a wall. He stays to

chat with me while I'm getting changed. I put my baby blue sweater and jeans back on in front of him. He tells me about American football and his three-year-old son. He leaves while confiding he's looking forward to seeing me again. I call Raymond and let him know my shift's over.

I hop into a taxi on Sherbrooke Street and head back home, with about $500 in my Lululemon gym bag. I divide the entire amount among three white envelopes, one with rent written on it in ink, another for laser hair removal, and the third for buying knee-high boots with high heels.

Debbie calls me the next day to inquire if I liked my first shift, I tell her I did, and she lets me know I must give her my schedule one week in advance. I look through my planner and offer to do two day shifts a week, from 9 A.M. to 5 P.M., Tuesdays and Thursdays, and one evening shift on Saturday. I don't want to work two consecutive days in order to keep my pussy from getting too sore and my jaw from getting too tired from smiling and sucking dick.

The following Tuesday morning, I get to the building, having eaten only half a blueberry muffin. I call Debbie when I arrive, and she tells me another girl, Mercedes, is already using apartment 708. I head towards apartment 408 on the fourth floor, the key's hidden inside a small magnetic box below the fire alarm. A basket full of bed sheets needing to be folded is waiting for me on the kitchen counter. I apply concealer under my eyes, on my nose, and forehead, use a bit of eyeliner, and finish with golden lip gloss. I get dressed up as a house maid. A girl knocks at the door, a small blonde girl with rosy cheeks and boobs jacked up by a burgundy velvet corset. I let her in, and she introduces herself in a peppy yet tired voice, "I'm Mercedes, are you new? I've been with Debbie for two years, I can make $300 today, do you fuck blacks? I don't. My favorite clients are big and full of tattoos. My boyfriend's in jail for a few months, he's covered in tattoos. I miss him, it's the second time he's in jail, did Debbie tell you? I met him because of his son. Can I borrow two or three towels, there aren't any clean ones at the apartment. I'll order some seafood pizza around noon, we can share it if you want, just don't forget your cell phone."

I thank her, curious to know more about her boyfriend in prison, but there's no way I'm going to share a pizza with her. I brought some radishes with me, which will be the only thing I'll have before heading back home. I don't want to have to make myself throw up to stay thin. I try to check the amount of calories in everything I eat. My first client arrives at 11, I had fallen asleep. There's dry drool on one of my cheeks. I quickly get cleaned up, chewing mint-flavored gum to change my breath from a lazy girl's dressed up as a maid to that of a lively escort. A guy in his thirties, with a British accent, tells me I'm cute and belong only to him for an hour. He picks me up and drops me on the bed. I immediately find him irresistible. I decide then the perfect guy has to be strong, British, and have dark eyes. We kiss, I unzip his pants and find him already hard. I take him in my mouth, I want to suck his bare dick, he strokes my hair, and his dick swells even more against my cheek. When I look at him, I find he has calm and soothing eyes. I could suck his cock for hours, but he wants to be deep inside my warm pussy. He sits me down on him, my back turned to him. My thighs hurt, I'm either not enough of a porn star or I lack experience. Samuel does me missionary style a bit too often.

He asks me to fellate him some more. I take off the condom, throwing it in the trash can, proud I got it on my first shot. I let my long black Pocahontas hair rest on his chest, like sexy actresses do in movies, before hiding their faces underneath the blankets, pretending to be sucking another super sexy actor. I continue my blow job, he tells me he's about to come, I want to keep him in my mouth and

I swallow it all. He seems surprised and thanks me. I then understand that escorts swallowing are pretty rare. He gives me a $50 tip. I bid him good day, he says he's off to visit his grandmother, and I find him even cuter, going off to brush my teeth. I want my breath to smell of mint and not cum when I kiss my next client.

Debbie warns me another client will be there in five minutes and another one at 1 P.M. I remove all the hairs from the bed sheets and make the bed while she's telling me, "I have to go to the pet shop, I want to buy new aquarium accessories, I have some big rocks, but I don't like them anymore, I think I'll try to find a little bridge and a plastic crab, and some lilac or mauve rocks so it'll shine at the bottom of the aquarium. I have to drive for an hour to get to my favorite pet store, it's a nuisance but I'm pretty sure I'll find some lilac or mauve stones there, and maybe another aquarium, I don't know where I could put it, but I like them, maybe I should redecorate my living room, move some armchairs, make room for another aquarium." I roll my eyes, listening to her, wondering if she's on antidepressants or speed or if she takes Cognac in her morning coffee. I interrupt her, hearing the next client at the door. She goes on, "I think he's Asian. You'll see we get a lot of Asian men as clients, I put up lots of ads in the Chinatown papers."

A very elegant Japanese man, his face hollowed by wrinkles, stretches out his lips to give me a kiss. I kiss him and guide him towards the bedroom. I jerk him off while he talks to me, and I have to ask him to repeat almost everything because I don't understand a word coming out of his mouth, but I continue smiling and nodding. He gets on top of me, holding my wrists down with his hands, and flicks his tongue in my mouth. I don't like his kisses and want to turn my head away from his mouth, give him my cheek or neck to kiss, but I don't. When he leaves, he gives me his business card. I think he wants me to call him sometime, he'd take me out to a restaurant, introduce me to his friends, and then we'd go dancing till midnight. Standing three feet away from him, my arms folded on my chest, I tell him I cannot see clients outside of work and I like my job too much to risk problems with the agency.

Until 5 P.M., I get dick after dick in me; a Brazilian guy working in a music studio on Laurier Street puts two fingers up my ass, and a close-to-retirement lawyer gives me a spanking. I put my envelope full of bills inside the little safety deposit box and wait for the girl working the evening shift, Sophie, in her thirties, with long brown curly hair and zits hidden under two coats of ivory-colored concealer, to arrive. She says, "I hope I'll have a lot of clients, it's like I'm going through withdrawal. I feel like a virgin again. I couldn't work for three days because I had burned my cheek with a straightening iron. I looked like a battered woman, my clients would have complained for sure." I sympathize with her. I'm also clumsy, likely to drop a box full of condoms on the escalator in the subway. I tell her I hope she'll get fucked all night and she blows me a kiss while lighting a cigarette.

I bump into Mercedes in the elevator and we leave the building together, me with my lime-and-lemon-colored gym bag, her clutching a Dora the Explorer backpack. She asks me if she smells bad. "My last client was sweating so much, he smelled like pea soup, and kept on badmouthing the Americans who reelected Bush." She stops in front of a parked car and exclaims, "Fuck, another ticket!" She lets go of her Dora the Explorer backpack and takes her cell phone out, hoping Debbie will agree to pay the fine.

I say goodbye to Mercedes and walk to the Eaton Centre, a shopping mall open till 9 P.M. every night. I want to buy underwear every color of the rainbow and padded bras. I go into La Senza. I stare at my naked reflection in the dressing room, touching my breasts the way clients did all day. I look for teeth marks or any kind of bruise, but can't find any, even my ass stopped being red despite the lawyer's spanking. I find myself pretty and would consider masturbating while staring at my reflection, with a tiny vibrator shaped like a tube of lipstick. I try on a bright pink satin bra and another peach-colored one with a boyish pair of lace underwear. I love how my ass looks in these boyish panties. I also buy a few black G-strings. I then sip a banana-chocolate smoothie while looking at the price of Matt & Nat handbags.

I go back to my apartment, wearing loose jeans, worn-out underwear, and a white blouse. Though I look like a sex bomb at work, I don't feel like making an effort when I go out, I don't want people noticing me. I can wear the same blouse all week, or dress like a dirty chic hippie as one of the Olsen twins does. My boyfriend hasn't complained so far. I don't remember the last time I did the dishes wearing only thigh-highs. As long as I'm prettier than the other students he rubs shoulders with and prettier than the shaved-head lesbians he works with at the restaurant, I won't worry and I'll spend my evenings with him, not wearing any makeup, my hair in a ponytail, playing Scrabble with him or telling him about the money I put in my envelopes hidden inside sugary cereal boxes.

# Things One Should Say to a Client

1. "Do you want me to use my mouth to put the condom on?"

2. "I touch myself at home, thinking about your dick."
(The client will believe it, especially if the escort keeps her eyes open and screams like Monica Bellucci in How Much Do You Love Me?)

3. "My ass is only yours."
(That way he feels special, but also the escort can charge more money.)

4. "I study anthropology."
(Or psychology, or mathematics, whatever. As long as the escort knows how to use grammatically correct sentences, the client feels he's doing a good deed and feels less guilty about cheating on his wife.)

5. "I go to the doctor every month for some tests. My left ovary's bigger than my right, but I'm free of all sexually transmittable diseases."
(Obviously, one should not only say this but also do it. It reassures the client who won't fear getting a life-threatening disease when the escort's saliva touches the tip of his penis.)

6. "Your wife should treat you better."
(Female solidarity? Who cares when the client's a good tipper.)

7. "Thank you so much, it was great."
(Then close the door, count and kiss the bills the client's just given you.)

8. "Tomorrow's my birthday. I'm turning twenty."
(To be repeated wholeheartedly until the age of thirty.)

9. "I hope you don't mind, I get really wet."

10. "I hate my dress. Can you tear it? While I'm on you? Getting off for the fifth time in thirty minutes, while pinching my nipples and yelling your name?"
(Only to be said to clients who tip well.)

# January Spent Playing a Barbie Full of Cum and Vitamin C

I watch five episodes of *NipTuck* before going to bed. I just love Kimber, the model redone twenty times turned porn star. I tell Samuel, "I want to have a blow-up doll just like Kimber, true to my body, that you could fuck all the time. I'd take baths with her and paint her nails. But I want thinner cheeks and Lindsay Lohan's nose." I can't close my eyes. I wake Samuel and ask him to talk to me about anything, to reassure me, to tell me I'm a better kisser than his exes, that all the other girls are fatter than me. I hammer the mattress, get up and drink lemon-flavored hot water, and look at the falling snow. I feel like going outside in the parking lot, naked, and freeze. I can't feel a thing tonight, except hate for myself, not sure why, maybe it's because I don't have Kimber's body or because I don't know how to love Samuel right. I thought being with him would prevent me from doing stupid shit, I thought his love would be enough, and I could start dreaming of starting a family with him. I thought I'd learn how to make lasagnas and knit wool caps complete with a pompom, I thought his friends would love me and I'd love his friends without being curious about the size of their dicks. I love Samuel, even after three years, but he doesn't bite me, slap me, pull my hair, or kindly mistreat me in any way when I say stupid things. I need a man who'd make me forget I'm as lost as Marissa in the TV show *The O.C.*, who could tell me if it's right or wrong to spend my days spreading my legs in bed. Or maybe a guy who simply wouldn't accept it.

I pet Porcelaine and bring her with me to bed, feeling her purring against my belly, and I cry. I refrain from waking Samuel again, despite wanting him to fuck me longer than clients do, telling me the same things they do. I fall asleep only to wake up from a nightmare five hours later on all fours.

I go to the grocery store by our apartment, next to a police station and a pawnshop, to buy some *pain au chocolat* and almond croissants. The stores are just opening. I stare at puppies in a pet-shop window and decide to go in. I wanted to be a veterinarian when I was twelve and write crime novels on the weekend. I thought life would be easy because so far everything was easy for me. I had the highest grades in my class, though sporting a perm no one dared make fun of me, I was very skinny and did ballet recitals with yellow flowers in my hair. I was the girl who could run faster than most boys. I made believe my golden retriever was a pony. My mother baked doughnuts from scratch and chocolate cakes and afterwards would give me the bowl to lick. My best friend stole eye pencils from the dollar-store Dollarama and gave me all her gossip magazines. When I was sixteen, I was a lifeguard at the municipal pool, despite my small breasts, the girl who sang Spice Girls' songs at the front door of her private school, the girl who could do it all, as they would often remind me. I wanted to be a veterinarian in the countryside and write crime novels, and now I get thousands of guys fucking me without being able to tell if I'm cuter than my cousin or my best friend.

I pet a big black cat that is wandering around the pet-shop, lost in my thoughts while the owner shows me his iguana in the back of the store. I want to give him my résumé, but I prefer smelling like sperm and latex than like bird shit and I don't think I'd want to work for $10 an hour. The list I keep in my Paperblanks notebook is getting longer every day. I giggle in front of the baby rats and a black and white one sticks out its tongue and licks my finger. I buy it and forget about the pastries.

Samuel's reading the newspaper *La Presse* at the table, with a bowl of café au lait, when I get back with the rat in the pocket of my fur-trimmed black coat. I put the rat down on his open newspaper and explain, "I fell in love. I don't know if it's a boy or a girl, his balls haven't dropped yet, but I think Gontran would be a nice name for it. Rats are super kind, my mom had a student who did his oral on domesticated rats, more sociable than hamsters, you could even bring Gontran to class, hidden in your school bag. Seriously, it's very decorative, we could put its cage underneath Sam Taylor-Wood's laminated portrait."

I take Gontran to the bedroom with me and put it in a shoebox. I text a friend to see if she wants to go out with me tonight and she replies that she plans to have a beer at Boudoir with some acquaintances of mine. She invites both Samuel and me. I take a nap, try twenty thousand different outfits, a Chupa Chups lollipop in my mouth, finally opt for some skinny jeans and an almost completely see-through black shirt, and go braless. I apply some Nuxe Huile Prodigieuse Or on my neck and chest and some black eyeliner around my eyes.

On the street, I don't hold Samuel's hand, always thinking I could bump into a client, and look nothing like a whore. I don't want to be in love anymore, or use Samuel as a five-foot-ten teddy bear. I need him but I also need other men, other dicks, bigger and harder than his, and lots of $100 bills. I know I'm getting to be a pain in the ass refusing to hold his hand or telling him how each dick tastes in my mouth, but I can't help myself.

At Boudoir on Mont Royal Street, I kiss everyone, checking to see if the barman's cute, order a vodka-cranberry, and sit next to Molly. She asks if I lost weight, and I tell her I didn't. I stare at her lips, I love Molly. I've been trying to convince her to take ecstasy with me and Samuel for months. It would be my first time doing ecstasy and I picture myself licking her for hours while watching my boyfriend fuck her. She has round baby cheeks, her breasts are barely bigger than mine, and I'm dying to know if she baby shaves her pussy or if she only leaves a line of hair to look like a landing strip.

I drink too fast. I rarely have alcohol and like only amaretto shots and vodka-cranberries. The first time I got drunk, I was fourteen. I had eight beers in three hours, did snow angels, and some acne-ridden guy held my hair while I puked in a sink before kissing me. Since then, I only drink once a month, and at Christmas, and on my parents' anniversary.

I don't care for the conversation. Caroline talks about her super annoying stepfather and the two Hermès scarves she inherited from her grandmother. I can't drink Cosmopolitans like the girls in *Sex and the City* do, all I think about is going back home in a cab, ordering Chinese food, and watching TV in the dark. I find everyone to be such a bore. I like my clients and their dicks better than Martin's history of Congo class or Kate's new hair color. I ask Molly to come to the bathroom with me. I let her know how bored I am and tell her I really want to kiss her. She refuses, "That's stupid, there's no one here to watch us." I'm surprised, I thought she liked me, but I now understand that my glossy lips are worthless if there's no guy around to stare at them.

I leave, bidding everyone good night, and Samuel follows me outside. I yell, "I hate everyone, and my best friend Misha is way prettier than Molly, and she's okay with kissing me anywhere, on the subway, in the library, but Molly's a real bitch who doesn't want to kiss me because there's no guy to turn on three inches away." Samuel strokes my hair until I fall asleep and the following morning, my face full of Super Restorative Wake-Up Clarins lotion, I swear never to drink again and to get new girlfriends.

I spend the weekend baking strawberry-marshmallow pies, watching Samuel roll his joints, doing sit-ups in front of *Nip/Tuck* episodes and playing with myself while thinking about Molly and one of my former drama teachers. When I wake up Monday morning to go to work, my face buried in Samuel's chest, my chin full of saliva, I feel like staying against him a few more minutes. I don't want to go to work, my pussy's a bit sore, and I have a headache. I touch Samuel's sack. I'd like him to force me to stay in bed with him all day, but he grunts and rolls onto his side away from me.

I get up and swallow Omega-3, vitamin C, and zinc tablets. I hop into the shower and distribute shaving cream on my legs, armpits, and pussy. I spread my ass cheeks to remove all hair around my hole. My hair still wet, I sip some green tea. I apply Hydra Zen lotion from Lancôme on my eyes and face. I stick whitening strips on my teeth and I leave with my Lululemon gym bag and the latest issue of *Elle Québec*. I repeat to myself, "What would Paris Hilton do?" and decide she would choose to have fun, stop complaining about her headache, and buy new flats and Chanel nail polish after work.

I look at well-dressed men on the subway, wondering which ones fuck whores. Brandon, Debbie's son, opens the door of apartment 408 for me. He tells me he hasn't slept all night, he was in a wrestling match, while showing me a picture of him in his wrestling gear taken with his cell phone. He's wearing a purple and black mask. "I won, and then I did

49

coke with two female friends. I fucked one for six hours, it's always long with me, she was almost sleeping when I was doing her up the ass, want to see a photo?" He watches me change into a puffy red miniskirt and a white camisole while drinking coffee. "I'm a DJ in a stripper club, you have a nice body, let me know if you want to dance, or if you want some pills, or if you want to suck my dick." I giggle and throw him out of the apartment, assuring him, "I'm already gonna be full of cum from the clients your mother sends, honey." Brandon doesn't worry me, I don't mind that he wants to sleep with me, he's funny and he knows he won't be able to get all his mother's whores to kneel down before him.

My first client's at the door, so I pee in a hurry, give myself one last look in the mirror, and answer. He's Italian, in his forties, and looks like Tony, the head of a mafia family on the TV show *The Sopranos*. He stays thirty minutes with me, and keeps his black Dolce & Gabbana T-shirt on while I'm on top of him, fucking him cowgirl style. He tells me he's going to Miami for a week to swim with dolphins and get loaded, he promises he'll come see me when he gets back, with a tan and a designer handbag. I take him in my arms. A guy in a Kanuk winter coat follows him, he doesn't get me wet at all, too skinny. He wants me to suck his dick without a condom and tells me he can only give me a $20 tip. I accept, though specifying he cannot come in my mouth or on my face. He ejaculates while I suck his tiny balls.

I read my horoscope in *Elle Québec*, call Samuel and ask him to pay the telephone and gas bills while using a cucumber-scented spray to hide the smell of sperm and sweat in the room. The man who looks like Mickey Rourke is back. I stroke his tattoos, he has a sun on his back and a yin-yang on his forearm. He'd like to own a laser clinic to remove flower tattoos from girls' ankles and have enough money to retire at fifty, settle in the countryside, and own a dozen energetic dogs. I lower his pants and just before licking the tip of his penis, I confide in him I have the same dream. He tells me he had a Great Dane when he was seventeen that was five-eleven on his hind legs. While I suck his cock, he twists strands of my hair around his fingers, telling me he's about to see Oasis live for the fifth time. I get down on all fours on the bed, his cell phone rings, and he penetrates my pussy for two minutes before reaching an orgasm, his hands spreading my ass so he can stare at my bum-hole.

An Indian man arrives while I'm eating a dozen almonds in front of the TV. His body's shaved and when I lie on top of him it itches. Because he has a huge cock, I let lots of lubricant drip onto my pussy. He fucks me for a good half hour and I end up telling him I want to see him come, tired from feeling his cock tearing my insides. He offers to do me standing against the wall. I smile, unsteady on my five-inch heels, and I stick my face against the eggshell wall. He puts his hands around my neck and asks what my real name is. I tell him, "Mélodie," which he says is much nicer than Marissa. After I watch him get dressed, we talk about McGill University, where he studies finance but would rather have been an actor. He tongues my ear lobe and gives me a $30 tip. I thank him. He says, "Do you want a boyfriend? Do you really need that much money?"

I close the door behind him and sigh, I don't know what I want, I need the money because I don't know what I'll do after, when men won't want me anymore. I save up to buy useless things like Tory Burch shoes but also for when I won't be able to live off sex, when I'll be alone in my apartment with my cats, weeping while reading *Cosmopolitan* because my hair is not glossy and straightened with an iron and I don't have a $500 bracelet sold exclusively at Bergdorf Goodman. I want to be an escort for two or three years and then have a little girl who'll play Barbies with me and speak

English before her first birthday. She'll become an actress or a diplomat later and I'll love her more than anything and she'll love me more than anything.

I'm opening my Paperblanks notebook to write the names of my morning clients when a piece of yellow cardboard falls from it. It's a note from Samuel, his calligraphy's prettier than mine, "Thanks Pussycat, for doing all you do for us. I wish you only clients with small penises. I love you. I'll wait for you at home with as many cheeseburgers as you can eat." Touched by his note, I look at my nails, tempted to bite them, I'd like to have time to call him and thank him and tell him I also only want small dicks and premature ejaculators. I put the piece of cardboard back in my notebook and entertain another client, my shiny eyes ready to cry if the guy's not talking to me as nicely as if I were a Disney princess.

He introduces himself, his name's Rodrigue, he pushes me towards the bedroom. I'm shivering all over. He's very sexy with his short gray hair and his Lucky 7 T-shirt. He throws his bills on the writing desk and grabs me, pulling my hair very hard. He bites my neck, I say nothing, and hitches up my red miniskirt. He licks my ass and penetrates it with his tongue. I bury my face in the comforter. He tries to put his dick in my ass, but I raise my head and say, "You have to put a condom on, and I want you in my pussy." He abruptly fucks me while I pinch my clit, he's really turning me on, and he comes before I have time to scream like porn stars do. He says, "I know you like it."

I'm still thinking about his depraved smile, his pale eyes, and his tongue when another client softly takes me by the hand. He puts his clothes on top of mine, along with his wallet and wristwatch. Having to give me an extra $50 for a condom-less blow job seems to embarrass him. I fellate him, staring at him with my half-closed eyes. I imagine I must have cute looks like that. He tells me he's about to come and

I finish him off between my 32A breasts.

He puts his gray wool sweater back on and I invite him to stay in bed with me. He tells me he doesn't like his job, he's an accountant, and wonders each day if he shouldn't become a sheep farmer or a pimp. He leaves, forgetting his watch on the dresser, of which I inform Debbie, but she doesn't have his phone number. I put the $100 along with the watch in the safety deposit box.

A forty-six-year-old hippie who lives on a catamaran in South America fucks me for two hours. I have a red face, flat hair, and a burning pussy when I get to my semiotic literature class at 6 P.M. I suck on a strawberry-flavored Chupa Chups and draw in my notebook. I hate students who ask lots of questions and the girls in the front row dressed in skinny jeans and cardigans. I'm tired, I just want to count the bills in my gym bag and go home. At the break, I hail a cab.

I jump into Samuel's arms when I get to the apartment and tell him I really want to drop out of school, that university's useless, and that I have no friends other than a poet who wants to sodomize me with lotion instead of lubricant and a punk chick with red hair whose breasts are almost bigger than Anna Nicole Smith's. Samuel looks at me with a scared look in his eyes and says, "Do what you want. But how will you explain it to your parents?" His stopping me disappoints me, though I'm really happy being the doll rich clients undress. I can't bear Samuel bringing me back to my state of little girl who must satisfy her parents.

I go online. I want to read what my clients are saying about me on MERB, a Website where men compare their experiences with Montreal masseuses, strippers, and escorts, while discussing hockey and asking various questions relating to sex, such as, "Has there been any cases of permanent blindness from Viagra use?" or "Is someone sexier with or without tan lines?" I am stressed out, I want everyone to love me. If a client gives me a bad review, many won't want to pay me for sex. I read a new comment, my knees coiled up against my chest. "She's very thin so you have to be gentle. When I touched her through her clothes, I could feel her getting wet. I became very hard and started licking her through her clothes, titillating her nipples. I sucked her small but firm breasts who got instantaneously hard, and I could hear her gently moaning. I had such a hard-on I couldn't wait, but she surprised me by saying, 'Let's go take a shower.' She smiled, took my hand and lead me to the bathroom. Before I continue, let me tell you that being with a girl who turns on the water and asks you if the temperature's good is, in my humble opinion, a real GFE.[1] So we took a shower and felt the hot water on our bodies. I could feel her hard flat belly and her piercing. I got down on my knees and flicked my tongue in her bellybutton. I looked up at her and offered her my most mischievous smile before putting a finger up her snatch. Oh God, she's really tight. She had such a fabulous look on her face when she came."

I shout at Samuel to come read this, only too happy to be seen as a GFE, an escort who's wonderful at pretending she's someone's girlfriend. And I never fake an orgasm. I remember that client, an Asian man who had about ten servings of General Tao too many in his belly, who had played with my clit while putting one finger up my pussy. With the hot water streaming down my body, I had found it so exciting I had an orgasm in the shower, just before he toweled me dry and gently fucked me in the bedroom. Samuel's lips are tightly shut as he reads the comment and I understand my blunder. He doesn't want to hear all the details of what I do with clients. As a matter of fact, he can't bear to know. I apologize and give him $50 so he can buy a new Nintendo GameCube

---

1. *Girlfriend experience*

game tomorrow, but also so he can recognize I spend hours in bed not only to satisfy my need for a future collection of a hundred pairs of high heels but also for us. I take a bath with rose and cardamom Bella Pella bubble bath and the wet Lucia Etxebarria's book *Love, Curiosity, Prozac and Doubts* in my hands. I stopped reading Don DeLillo or Dostoyevsky when I became an escort, needing lighter subject matter, and I want to laugh with Etxebarria's characters and imagine myself shopping in Spain during a heat wave. I love working for the agency, but secrets make me queasy. Only my cousin knows I'm an escort and we discuss it almost every Sunday, when we have breakfast at Cora's in the Gay Village, but all my friends and parents think I work in a call center.

Porcelaine, liking the heat, comes to sit on the edge of the bathtub. She rubs against the Redken shampoo bottles and the ladybug-shaped soap dish. I set *Love, Curiosity, Prozac and Doubts* down on the bathroom floor and put my head underwater. Porcelaine reaches for my nose with her paw.

I ask Samuel if he can bring me a cheeseburger and he accepts, as he accepts everything, never able to say he disagrees with me, even when I try to shock him with racist slurs. He brings a tray to the bathroom and sets it down. I open my mouth and say, "Want me to blow you, honey?" He replies by taking off his jeans and lobster-print underwear.

# Rolling on the Floor in Wet Black Panties

Today I'm working in Dorval for the second time, in a hotel room Debbie rents on a yearly basis. I do longer days in Dorval, staying in the room from 9:30 A.M. to 8:00 P.M., and I fuck at least ten guys because escort agencies are rarer in the West Island than downtown, and also because we're ten minutes away from an international airport. I take a bus from Lionel-Groulx metro station and call Debbie to let her know I'm on my way. She says she'll meet me at Dorval station to give me the hotel room key. "I'm stuck in Nun's Island traffic, it's horrible in the morning, get a coffee and wait for me."

Her spaniel's with her. He jumps on me and licks my face. I'm afraid I'll smell more like a hyperactive dog than of Givenchy's Very Irresistible perfume. Debbie lets me into the room. It's huge, with a balcony and lots of rolled-up white towels in a storage cabinet. Debbie tells me to leave the key and the money in the microwave.

I welcome my first client in a black velvet mini dress bought at the Goth store Cruella. His arms and back are full of burn scars. He tells me he just arrived in Montreal, "My second book is about the history of the Jews, I'm giving a three-day conference here." We lie down and I run my fingers down his body, caressing him and his scars which don't disgust me but arouse my curiosity. I wonder if many girls dare kiss and touch his ugly skin. We talk about World War II and how my face sometimes resembles Charlotte Gainsbourg's or Céline Dion's. He tells me he'll try to come see me again before leaving for Germany, and I give him our downtown address where I'll be working in two days.

I close the door behind him and look through the peephole at a group of flight attendants, with identical luggage on wheels, walking down the corridor in front of my room. I channel-hop through all the available TV stations at least three times before another client arrives. He looks at me and says, "I wanted to see Diana, the Puerto Rican girl, do you know her? She's the only one I fuck, but Debbie told me she was working downtown today and that's too far for me. I hope you like giving blow jobs because I really need a dirty girl to suck my prick without a condom. I don't give Diana any tip, I bring her presents." He takes a box with a brand new blow dryer out of a garbage bag and another box containing a straightening iron. He asks me if I need a round brush as well. I don't like his abruptness but promise myself I'll behave.

He washes his hands in the banana-yellow bathroom. He tells me to bring him a new towel and dry his hands. I do so, but he says I'm not considerate enough and am doing it too fast. He throws me a, "Diana does everything better than you. Now blow me!" in my face. I find him unfair. I am no longer making the effort to smile, knowing I'll never see him again after today. I lick his penis, my tongue going underneath his balls and mechanically exploring the tip of his penis. When I look up at him, he's staring at his reflection in the bathroom mirror. I warn him that I don't swallow. He grunts, "I'll come in your face." I'm about to refuse when I think about the straightening iron he brought me that must be worth $150, so I accept, sticking a few stray locks behind my ears.

I reapply my makeup after making sure my nose and cheeks are sperm-free. And I'm surprised to see Pierre, Tony Soprano's lookalike. He usually only visits me downtown, often twice a week. He tells me he dreamt of me the night before, that he missed me too much and that his life isn't going well. He fought with his wife, who spends all her time with soccer moms and gold-diggers and has been sleeping at her brother's for the last couple of days. I hug him and promise I'll do my best to make him forget it all for the next thirty minutes. I bring him to the bedroom, which seems to make him nervous. He looks at the half-open closet door, "What's in it? A camera?" I tell him only my clothes and my gym bag. I open the door, show him my jeans and my violet cross-over top, and all the empty coat hangers. He asks me if I'm a hundred per cent sure there's no camera. I try to reassure him that the agency wouldn't film its clients, that the girls would feel threatened.

He touches my dress with his fingers, "It's so soft, just like you, honey." He lies down on the bed and asks me to straddle him. I jerk him off and once he's hard again, I give him a condom, still no good at putting them on. He tells me Sophie can put one on with her mouth; he saw it on the MERB Website. To which I reply, "No way! She's my new idol!" Once I'm on top of him, he climaxes in no time while stroking my tits. I wish him a good day; he calls me "princess" and kisses me before hiding his eyes behind Gucci shades.

I look at the time and decide to lie naked on the bed, while starting my homework about the meaning of strippers in Victor-Lévy Beaulieu's[2] work. Debbie calls me forty minutes later, while I am staring at my nails wondering if I'd let Victor-Lévy Beaulieu bite my ass cheeks. I put my books on the living room table, so clients can see them. Guys

---

2. Quebec playwright and novelist active since the late 1960s

love student escorts, they feel like they're helping a young respectable girl pay for her education instead of paying a slut addicted to hard drugs.

A smiling and super sexy guy knocks at the door, I open, he looks at me and spins me around, making me giggle. I take his coat off and put it on an armchair. He whistles. "You're really skinny, I love it, you'll be my little thing, I don't get guys who like bigger girls, it's waifs that make me hard, I love your collarbones, can you show me your belly?" I raise my dress up to my pierced bellybutton adorned with a silver ring.

I undress in the bedroom and he cuddles with me in front of a tall mirror. He touches me. "Your small ass. Your back. How much do you weigh?" I feel like one of the Olsen twins or like a fifteen-year-old Calvin Klein model. I stare at my reflection in the mirror, "I don't know, I never step on a scale, around a hundred pounds, I think." My client tells me he could crush me and hear my bones snap, because he's a giant next to me. I've only been part of the Dream&Cream agency three months and I've lost five pounds from sweating while fucking and eating only one meal a day and fruits every hour. I'm really proud of having to wear a belt with my twenty-three-inch-waist Guess jeans.

We fuck, my legs resting on his shoulders and he comes with the same smile he had on his face when he entered the hotel room. Debbie calls to let me know my next client will be there in two minutes. I remind my muscular giant to pay me before leaving and he gives me a $50 tip, making me promise never to gain any weight.

I drink a few sips of raspberry-flavored water to rehydrate, and apply some lip balm. I feel super happy and want to dance like a little girl in front of the mirror. I've always been thin, but in elementary school the kids called me "celery-legs." I wasn't too proud of my little breasts, but today, thanks to them, I earn a living as the 32A prepubescent doll escort.

A fifty-something man in a perfectly pressed three-piece suit kisses me, then squints at me and says, "Gorgeous, do you know what would please me?" I say no. He strokes my hair and adds, "I'm married so I'd like you to take a shower so I won't smell of your perfume. Also remove your makeup so it won't stain my shirt." I find it really annoying having to wash ten times a day, probably making my skin really dry, but I do it. The hour I have to spend with him will go faster if I stay in the shower ten minutes touching myself.

When he penetrates me with his small dick, his glasses resting on the bedside table, I think about Natacha Merritt's photo album. I'll soon reward myself with a toucan-shaped almond pastry. I allow myself one dessert a week, and when the following client talks about the CBC[3] radio shows he listens to, I think about the fact I need to buy lubricant at the drugstore and extra-thin Japanese condoms that another escort recommended. I'm tired, it's dark outside, and I stick my feet on the heater.

A guy with brown hair who looks like a teacher's pet with his forest green polo shirt kisses both my cheeks and asks to stay an hour with me. We sit in front of the TV, and as the news repeats I suggest we turn it off or go to the bedroom. I feel like I'm seventeen, trying to fuck a friend who'd rather have me apply lipstick on his lips. Feeling nervous, I'm afraid the guy might jump me, forcing me to give him a clown make-up. I try not to play with my nails and put my hand down his beige pants. He holds my hand against him and I can feel him getting hard. Either politely or shyly he asks me if it's okay for him to take off his pants and Tommy Hilfiger underwear. I say yes, and he sits back down on the armchair, still wearing his polo shirt, his big

_____

3. Canadian Broadcasting Corporation, national public radio

dick pointing at me. I go get condoms and blow him while he strokes my hair. I sometimes check the time on the TV, and forty minutes later, when the guy comes one finger up my pussy, my mouth is quite numb. He thanks me, saying he can never ask his girlfriend to suck his dick because it takes him too long to climax, but he really enjoys it. I stand on tiptoe and gently kiss his mouth. I'm quite surprised, he looks like he's thirty and I thought all thirty-something men came within ten minutes in my mouth. I hope he'll come see me again. He's nice and thanks to him, my pussy can rest for an hour.

I start chewing mint-flavored gum while looking at my hair. I find it dull. I'm due for another Clairol coloring. I call Samuel and hang up at the sound of my recorded voice on the answering machine and call back until he picks up. I ask him to wait for me to eat, we could order some Vietnamese food and rent an action film, though I hate our rental store. The last time I went, an old man wanted to give me a palm reading and scared me by telling me I was going to die young and should do Transcendental Meditation.

A guy with very short gray hair arrives, who I think might be in a cooking show. He asks for thirty minutes. He follows me to the bathroom. I give him a facecloth and he wipes his dick while telling me he's going to meet friends at a new wine bar. I shamefacedly confide in him that I know absolutely nothing about wine, and he tells me he'll bring me a bottle of his favorite wine next time to arouse an interest in me for things other than vodka-based cocktails.

Dancing to Nelly's music video *Hot in Herre* on TV, I admire black dancers' asses before entertaining another client, an amateur pilot who tells me all about his last trip to an almost deserted island and leaves chewing black licorice. It's almost 8 P.M., I tidy up the room and make sure I placed the correct amount inside the microwave. Just when I'm ready to put my jeans and violet cross-over top on, Debbie lets me know I have one last client. This means I'll miss the bus and have to wait half an hour for the next one, but Debbie says I should let Brandon drive me home.

My client made me happy, fucking while spooning. He had hurt his leg and this was the only position that did not give him any pain. We talked about hockey and he gave me $600 instead of $200 because he thought I was sweet and only sees escorts once or twice a year. Brandon takes me home forty minutes later. In Brandon's black BMW, I stay quiet, mentally calculating if I should get laser hair-removal or put money aside in case I catch the flu before the winter's finished. Brandon talks on his cell phone; he's going to meet Sophie and Cinnamon, another escort, at the Green Room on St. Laurent Street. He tells me he went to visit a friend in jail today and so he needs to get drunk. He used to steal from convenience stores and gas stations with his friend and never got caught, but his friend will be behind bars for the next two years. I don't ask why, waiting for him to tell me, but he only shakes his head, his long hair hiding his face.

I tell him he can drop me off at the metro station nearest to the bar but he assures me he'd be pleased to drive me home even if it's far. He asks me about my other clients and my boyfriend, then he gets another call and writes down an address. "Tomorrow I'll have to break down the door of another agency. You know there's already several downtown but there's a new one now, I don't know who opened it, and when that happens I pretend I'm a client but I arrive there early and break down the door, scaring the girl and her client if she's with one, then I tell her to tell her boss I came by. If the agency continues its operations, I go back and destroy all that's inside, take the girl's money, and warn her next time I'll rape her, which I wouldn't do, but I have to tell her that so she'll know I'm serious and won't accept another agency setting up." I pretend I agree with him, but imagining another unlucky escort face to face with a muscle man threatening to explode her hole terrifies me.

Back at the apartment, I throw my money in the air like they do in movies, but I'm disappointed to see that even $1,000 in $20 bills is not enough for me to roll in bills on the floor while fake-screaming like a porn star. Samuel can't believe the money I made and I ask him to order from *La Merveille du Vietnam*. I want some pineapple chicken, hold the sweet and sour sauce.

Having the next day off, I get up late and read the newspaper *La Presse* in bed while drinking lots of green tea. Then I go to the drugstore to buy some hair color, Redken conditioner, Venus razors, lubricant, a box of thirty-six condoms, and I invite my mother to come see me since I'll be spending the evening alone. Samuel works until 10 P.M. My mother and I used to fight all the time, over stupid things like the length of my skirts or because I accused her of liking my brothers better. As a kid, I was always happy, but my teenage years were tough and I was miserable. I listened to Tori Amos non-stop and cut my wrists with kitchen knives. My parents worried so much about me they forced me to keep my bedroom door open, hoping to prevent me hanging myself or masturbating while staring into Marilyn Manson's eyes. Since I became an escort, I feel calmer, no longer full of anxieties, and I no longer get up in the morning wanting to throw it all away, drop out of school, not pay my rent, and steal the neighbor's car and drive to Mexico. My mom and I talk almost an hour on the phone. She needs to get up early the next morning because she plans to go skiing with her sister, so she prefers not driving to Montreal. I let her know Samuel and I found a new apartment and we'll be moving soon. She seems happy for me and I tell her she's going to love the new apartment, which is located on St. Denis Street, on top of a beauty salon next to a subway station where people don't deal drugs. I explain in detail what all the rooms look like and what color I'll paint the walls.

Samuel finds me asleep on the couch, wearing only a bustier and black panties. I jump into his arms, telling him I want to give him a lap dance, having practiced for an hour and a half on a Christina Aguilera song he doesn't like and made myself up like a cabaret star. He puts a pizza down on the living room table and sits down while I select the song and approach him, spreading his legs and rubbing against his chest and dick. I slowly undo my bustier's clips and caress my tits, saying, "I'd love to be able to excite you by licking my boobs but even if I pull really hard on them, I can't, my breasts are too tiny. Do you want to lick or bite them?" I jerk him off while singing along and he climaxes in my hand, telling me I'm the most beautiful girl in the world. I ask him to promise he'll always love me, and he does. I hug him and thank him. I make him smell my black undies and go play with myself in the bedroom, behind a closed door.

Later in the week, I'm working downtown, and one evening I'm heartbroken at the thought of leaving the apartment. Porcelaine, who I noticed had recently gained weight, gave birth that very morning under the covers, continually meowing, huddled against me. I look at her with her newborn kitten all black and sticky and I have to run to the metro with my Lululemon bag, sad that I have to abandon Porcelaine like this. When I thought she was stealing Syphilis' food she was actually carrying that ugly cat's babies.

I knock at the door of apartment 408 and Amber, an escort who looks like Scarlett Johansson, opens the door, her eyes red from crying. She's with Vera, a redhead who's always stuffing Snickers bars down her throat. Vera lights a cigarette and offers me one while explaining why Amber seems discouraged. "A client recognized her this afternoon. She was with her mother and little brother. And the asshole, instead of smiling at her or doing nothing, waved at her, calling her 'Amber!'" Amber continues, pulling at her baby pink and blue schoolgirl skirt, "I didn't turn around, I was putting bags in the trunk of my car, but the guy must have thought I didn't hear him because he started tapping my shoulder and asking how I'm doing, the fucker! I turn around, recognize him, give him the eyes, hoping he'll understand this is not the right moment since I'm next to my mother. But the guy's thick and says something like, 'Sorry, Amber, I didn't mean to disturb you?' Shit, couldn't he have said he had mistaken me for someone else? Like I'm using my real name when I'm whoring. My mother was looking at me funny afterwards. I felt like shit, really. I don't feel like staying tonight. Can I stay here and watch TV with you, Marissa, until our first clients arrive?"

I agree, but don't know what to say to make her feel better. I'd feel so embarrassed and ashamed if my parents knew I pretended to be a doll for people to undress, several days a week, downtown. Vera strokes Amber's back. "I bumped into one of my clients at Canadian Tire,[4] he was with his wife. I saw another one on the metro. I kept my mouth shut. You just don't do that. You were really unlucky, Amber."

Vera shows us a bag that she left in the living room closet full of contraceptive sponges escorts use when they have their period and want to continue working. "Don't hesitate if you need any." She says she must leave because she has to meet people for a group project for her fashion marketing class. Amber hugs her then follows me to the living room. I don't know if I should change in front of her or retreat to the bathroom.

While Amber puts *Finding Nemo* into the DVD player,

---

4. Hardware and automotive store

after Oprah Winfrey's show just ended, I change the bed sheets and put my box of condoms and my lubricant on the bedside table, and store my makeup in the bathroom closet. I change in front of Amber, putting on a black skirt and a blouse which molds my small breasts. She tells me, "You're so skinny. I'd love to look like you, clients must love you, tattoo-free, you look like a perfect little girl. I must have at least a client a day telling me he hates the butterflies on my back."

I'm surprised to hear Scarlett Johansson complimenting me and I ask her to show me her tattoos. Amber stands up and removes her satin cami. Half her back's covered in monarch butterflies and there's a key on her left shoulder blade, a very big gray key.

I apply Nuxe's lotion full of golden flakes all over my chest. Amber borrows some and starts applying it, while I look at her, trying not to fantasize about her, thinking how sexy and beautiful she looks in her sex-shop costume. I hope a client will ask to be with two girls tonight. I picture myself gently spreading Amber's legs, her red face covered with Benefit foundation, and burying my face in her pussy. I'm sure it's shaven, soft, warm, and wet, even before someone tickles her clit with a finger. My cell phone rings before I have time to offer to lick her. Debbie lets me know Samir's on his way and should arrive within five or ten minutes. Even though I must ask Amber to leave and go back to her apartment six stories up, I'm really happy because I love Samir, who has a very large dick but can't always get it up with me, though always thanking me, telling me I'm touching and adorable once he's out the door, ready to leave me.

As soon as Samir arrives, I jump into his arms. He asks me what's new in my life and I tell him my cat Porcelaine gave birth next to me earlier in the day, that at first she was scared of her kitten and was circling it really fast, still attached to it though its umbilical cord, and I had to give her the kitten so she could clean it up and put it against her still pregnant belly. We lie down on the bed, he strokes my hair and tells me about the neighborhood where he grew up in Algiers, which was full of stray cats. In the building where his family used to live, there was an old lady who let her cat roam around the floors. A very intelligent cat, it meowed when it wanted to take the elevator. I find his anecdote amusing and I undo his pants and take his whole cock in my mouth while he continues talking about Algiers, then he stops talking and asks me to look at him while I blow him. He sits up on the bed, his back against the wall, his legs wide open. I go between his legs and smile at him. He touches my cheek so gently. I don't know why he thinks I'm adorable or touching but I love to hear him talk and I love his hand whether it's on my hair, cheek, or ass. He slowly gets hard and asks to penetrate me. I lie down on my back and he penetrates me, but after a few seconds I can feel him losing his hard-on. He kisses my breasts, licks my bellybutton, and takes the condom off, not saying a word. I like that he's not thinking up excuses for his limp cock, saying it's because he's exhausted or because of work or because my pussy's not wet enough. We discuss Philip K. Dick's novels and he writes a title down for me on a page of my Paperblanks notebook, a title I promise to buy and read very soon.

I jerk him off and he comes in my hand, just before Debbie calls, worried because I've been with Samir for more than an hour. When I don't have any other clients, I sometimes forget to check the alarm clock on the bedside table. I don't like thinking about the time and I don't want my clients to feel rushed. Samir kisses my forehead and tells me to take care. I wash myself with a facecloth and knock at Amber's apartment. She opens the door, putting her finger on her lips. She's on the phone, "Yes, Lilianne, I'll be done at the bar soon, I'll meet you guys at Stereo. I'll call you later. You'll die when you see my new shoes."

Amber sighs and puts her cell phone down on the white melamine kitchen table. "I'm going out after, I'll need to leave my stuff here, I brought a lock. Another girl stole Véronika's BCBG Max Azria dress. My friends think I work at a high-end gentlemen's club." She shows me her silver Roman sandals, "$300 at Miss Sixty." I open my mouth and say, "Oh, I want some like that!" I ask her how long she's been an escort and she says she's been back here working for Debbie for the last six months, she likes change and that way there are always clients eager to try the new girl. She goes to the bathroom, leaving the door open. I see her pee, sitting on the bowl with her schoolgirl skirt and her white panties down around her knees. "I might do some independent work soon, I don't know, my regular clients are boring me, there's a TVA[5] producer who was with me for half an hour before you got here, who always tries to get me to come to his place to watch old Claire Lamarche episodes, you know, the panel talk show where a little old lady says she's looking for her mother who abandoned her when she was, like, one because she had this ugly birthmark on her face. Well, now she got it removed and all she's got are lines on her face and some dentures, and all she wants is to find her nasty mother to thank her for giving her life and to ask if there's a history of breast cancer in the family." I laugh and say, "That's the man with the colored scarf, he gave me his business card too, he wanted to take me dancing to Buena Notte."

Amber gets a call, "No, I don't do blacks. Do you want to talk to Marissa?" Debbie asks me to go back to my apartment because a client should be there within ten minutes. I agree to see the client, though many girls don't want to do blacks, fearful of larger-than-the-norm dicks, afraid their pussy

---

5. Privately owned French-language TV network

might be sore for their next clients. Amber wishes me luck and I entertain a gorgeous and classy guy at my apartment. He asks me about my services and doesn't understand that I don't want to suck his bare dick for free. I don't like arguing, "That's how it is, I know some agencies offer that for free, but they charge more than us for an hour." I'm uncomfortable, feeling defensive, so I try to lighten things up by saying, "But you can put my panties all the way up my snatch if you want." He calls me a little slut, which makes me smile. He tosses me against the wall, gets undressed while rubbing against me, and I remind him he has to put on a condom. He grunts, "I'm not even in you yet, let me stroke you with my dick, tell me you want to feel it, you want to get it deep in you, little slut, do you want it?" I release myself from his embrace and bring back a condom. He masturbates in front of me to get even harder. He has an enormous cock, I pour a lot of lubricant on my pussy. He penetrates me and, just an inch in, my vagina tightens, I'm terrified, I'm already in pain. He tries to force me to continue by going in harder. I tell him to slow down, let me catch my breath, and he gets impatient. His hard-on diminishing, he takes off the condom and tries to penetrate me again. With an exhausted voice, I tell him I can't allow this. I stare at my plastic wedding ring with dried flowers inside and think very hard about Samuel.

I'm willing to blow the guy for free, anything not to feel his dick in my pussy, afraid I'll start bleeding if he goes any deeper. I feel bad for agreeing to see him. I don't need money that badly, I deposited $5,000 in my bank account two days ago and I have the same amount in white envelopes still hidden inside cereal boxes and the vegetable trays of my old fridge. The black man puts another condom on, comes between my legs and spits on my pussy, "Stop worrying, I won't hurt you, slut." And plunges into me. I see him trying to remove the condom after two, three, four in-outs, "I won't be able to come with that thing on my dick, it's too tight." I warn him I'll let Debbie know. He asks for his money back and I refuse, going on all fours, hoping my ass will be hot enough for him to reach a quick orgasm, without having to feel like I'm getting gang-banged by three dicks. He leaves after having explored my ass for forty minutes. I'm close to tears when I call Samuel and ask him if Porcelaine had any more babies. He informs me she had five more and I smile, telling him I might come home sooner than expected, that I had a really bad evening. I can't hold in my tears anymore, which really worries Samuel. I tell him not to panic, that for the first time I'm really in pain and I feel like taking my gym bag and my money and leaving this apartment without ever coming back.

I regain control of my emotions, stare at my reflection in the mirror for ten minutes, telling myself I'm pretty and that everything will be all right, and I hop into a hot shower. Debbie promises me my next client will be nice, and an Asian man arrives. He puts delay cream, preventing premature ejaculation, all over his shaft and I'm really starting to get discouraged, feeling like there's no way I can act like a bitch in heat for very long. The client's dripping sweat all over me and does me in twenty different positions. I make no effort whatsoever, I don't want to be on top, I don't want him putting a finger up my ass, I don't want him kissing me, I just want him to leave. I watch him walk towards the elevator, I lock the door behind me, and call Debbie, "Can I leave early? I'll pay whatever fee, but I'm in too much pain to continue working." Debbie lets me go, telling me to rest and put some ice on my pussy. She talks about a Garfield-shaped cake she wants to buy her dog and a penthouse in the Olympic Village's Pyramid she'll get for escorts earning higher hourly wages.

# Licking Asses to Forget I'm Jealous of Muffin-Top Girls

Samuel and I move at the beginning of April, a few days after celebrating my birthday at my parents'. I had asked my mother to make me a mango, avocado, and shrimp salad, and Samuel to buy me a Barbie doll. My parents are here today, to help us move, empty the fridge, fit all the kittens into a cage with a faulty lock, and lift all my heavy cardboard boxes full of books. I feel light hearted and ecstatic, as if moving to a new neighborhood will change my life and prove that I made the right choices.

The movers, friends of my dad's, start laughing when they see me dressed in skinny jeans and wearing high heels. Now that our former apartment's empty, I find it dirty and sad and don't understand how I lived in a basement apartment for a year without becoming an alcoholic like my neighbors or needing to take 500 mg of Zoloft. After seeing a guy show his dick in front of my kitchen window while I was doing dishes and finding a homeless woman sleeping in front of my door, I'm ready to leave and forget all the cab drivers calling me Hochelaga's princess[6] and the old wannabe fortune teller at the DVD rental store.

In my mother's car, I take note of all the things making

---

6. A reference to a well known local restaurant where waitresses are topless

me happy on the way to our new apartment; "An elementary school for when I'll have a little girl! A produce store with normal well-dressed clients! A pet shop for when Samuel will let me have a long-haired Chihuahua! A bakery! Oh Mommy, my new favorite bakery, we should go see it right away!" My mother's impressed by the apartment, located on St. Denis Street, right next to the Bleu Raisin restaurant and a beauty salon. She asks me how much I pay in rent. I pet Syphilis, who's terrified and doesn't stop meowing, and I lie, reducing the rent by $350, "Oh, we were really lucky to find this, it's only $600 a month."

The movers, my parents, Samuel, and Julien, one of his friends, spend the day emptying the truck, lifting boxes, and sweating while I'm waiting for the fridge, stove, washer, and dryer to be delivered, being careful not to break a nail opening boxes. My dad puts my IKEA shelves together and I start alphabetizing my books. I offer our helpers some extra large pizzas and cold beers but only Julien decides to stay. We listen to Arcade Fire and Opeth while Julien talks about his philosophy classes, guitar lessons he gives, and the first time he tried coke, a few days ago, with a girl he met at a metro station. The guys roll a joint while I light some candles, drinking only raspberry-flavored water. I feel like coiling up against them, telling Julien to touch my hair so he can notice how much shinier and softer my hair is than his ex's was, or my cousin's, with whom he had an affair last summer. Julien leaves around 2 A.M., borrowing my Samuel Beckett's *The Unnamable*, and Banana Yoshimoto's *Kitchen*, and Samuel gets a stressed look on his face when I hold Julien really tight and kiss him very close to his lips.

The next morning, I wake up late and ask Samuel to call in sick at work so we can go explore our new neighborhood. We walk to Fou d'Asie, an Asian restaurant close to the university. I buy Samuel lunch and we order unknown food and I laugh at him because he refuses to eat a piece of sushi. I have some tea and a soup that's much too spicy and I point at girls on the street, "Look at this one with her muffin top! She has ten pounds of overhanging fat spilling over the waistline of her jeans!" I ask Samuel about Sandrine, one of his colleagues he likes, whom I met a few times at the apartment, "Does she still cheat on her boyfriend? Does she still have a double chin? Does she still think she'll become a famous actress?" I can feel Samuel's hurt and I stop criticizing Sandrine. Every time he likes a girl, I can't help myself, I shamelessly run her down. I think I'm better than all the girls he knows just because I'm paid to be desired, but though I have no reason, I am jealous, because I can't believe he finds other girls interesting and because I know there must be a girl nicer than me, simpler to understand, who doesn't lie when she says she likes Mogwai's music and dozens of others with breasts big and round enough to tit-fuck.

I spill some soup on my Orange Crush T-shirt, which infuriates me. Samuel tries to calm me down, telling me he'll wash my T-shirt at the apartment so there'll be no trace of the stain, even if I were to drop the rest of my soup on it. My cell phone rings and I answer while blowing Samuel a kiss. I'm surprised to hear the voice of Fabrice, my former drama teacher, on the line. He wonders if I'd like to come over to his place tonight because he misses me, and I accept right away without thinking twice about what Samuel might think. I'm really excited at the thought of seeing Fabrice again. He once saw me put a bottle of nail polish remover up my cunt during a school play and that didn't stop him from fucking me in his office during the summer break, while he was alone in the department preparing his courses for the following semester.

I take a taxi to his place. I haven't seen him in months, and he tells me he just had his bike stolen, and feeds me orange slices on his balcony overlooking an elementary school and a rectory. He says he loves the back of my neck so I tie my hair up using the elastic I often wear around my wrist. He tells me he left Maude, says a few things about her: she liked popping his zits and having missionary-style sex. He asks me how it's going with Samuel, "I never imagined you'd fall for a guy like him. He's too nice. How did it start between you two?" I look at Fabrice and smile, "He's the first guy who ever kissed me. Can you believe it? I was in awe of him when I was thirteen, he was the best at mathematics and French and could sing English songs. We dated for two weeks and he broke up with me because he thought I was too clingy, we spent all our free time together, kissing and touching each other in the park by the school. He left me because he wanted to date one of my friends who didn't even like him and said he kissed like a dog, like a St. Bernard, you know, with too much tongue and saliva. He fell back in love with me when we were in CEGEP.[7] I spent all my Sunday evenings with him, after giving ski lessons to five year-olds." Fabrice offers me a glass of port. I accept and follow him to the kitchen, where I pour myself a glass of water and notice on his refrigerator door a newspaper clipping, an obituary. "She was one of my students. She killed herself. She tied bricks to her ankles and jumped in her parents' pool."

The glass of port seems to have taken his shyness away and he asks me how it's going at the agency. I listen to the sound of crickets hidden among the fir trees before answering him, with my eyes lowered, "I don't want to talk about it, Fabrice." He remains silent, it makes me uncomfortable, then I stand up and force him. "I burned myself, the other day, using hot wax for the first time, and I managed to burn myself below my buttocks, want to see? You can still see it. I

7.Specialization after high school, mandatory to complete in Quebec before going to university

apply lotion there every hour. I'm supposed to start working again this week." I lower my frilly gray mini. "I didn't rinse myself properly under the shower, some wax stayed on, and I got second degree burns. I'll never use hot wax again. My boss didn't even believe me when I told her my blunder. She thought I wanted to take some time off." Fabrice laughs, strokes my bum, "It could only happen to you." And puts a finger up my ass. I quiver gently and tell him we should head in.

In the hallway, he embraces me and puts his hand between my thighs. He pulls me to his bedroom and I read the title of the book he left on the bedside table, *A History of Reading* by Alberto Manguel, and I tease him about his messy bed, "Don't you make your bed in the morning?" I can see the Mont-Royal mountain from his room. He undresses and asks me to join him. I pretend I don't hear him when he asks if I'm happy he left his girlfriend. He asks me if I'd consider sleeping with both him and Samuel at the same time. I refuse, "But if you let me lick one of your female Asian students, then yes." He kisses me and I close my eyes, he lifts up my skirt and comes between my legs. He licks my skin while continuing to insert his fingers up my ass and then up my cunt. Before I get a chance to orgasm, he gets on top of me and puts his dick in my mouth. I can't breathe with his ass in my face. I lick his asshole and his balls, I suck on one of my fingers before gently inserting it in his ass, being careful not to hurt him with my very long nails. He makes a strange noise, like a cat purring, and tells me he's about to erupt. I tell him to ejaculate on my face, I want to feel his wet cum on my face. I stick my tongue out and manage to swallow a few drops. He gives me a tissue so I can wipe my cheeks and chin. It does me a world of good to make a man orgasm without having to ask him for money.

Fabrice takes a shower and comes back wearing navy blue pajamas. He lends me a sweater to wear underneath my spring jacket, which is not warm enough for these cold April evenings. We go back out on his balcony with cheese he wants me to try, and he tells me he knows actresses who'd kill to have sexy bedroom eyes like mine. He tells me he loved how I licked his asshole, and he thought he might be gay when he was thirteen because he let a friend's older brother blow him and insert fingers up his ass. "Now that guy fucks his female dog and sees a vet every month because of it." I yawn and he looks at me with tender eyes. He asks if I want to spend the night with him, I say no, that I have to get going, and he offers to drive me home.

Three days later, I'm working downtown, my skin still a bit red where the wax burned me, but not afraid clients might think I have a skin problem or that I let someone torture me. Diego, a very rich client always on business trips, is my first one of the day and he just wants to sleep the jetlag off with me. He's back from Japan and even though he has a hard-on, he doesn't want to penetrate me, just to cuddle for an hour. I have to fight to stay awake, despite being ultra comfortable, too afraid I might snore or drool on my client. I look at him, with his eyes closed, his light skin tone, and his barely lined forehead. He smells like chicken noodle soup.

He gives me his business card before leaving and I hug him for a long time. I pull the elastic on my panties and let it slap against my ass, and pretend I'm a sexy girl who knows how to dance, and sing Ciara's song *Goodies,* "I bet you want the goodies, bet you thought about it, got you all hot and bothered, maybe cuz I talk about it, lookin' for the goodies, keep on lookin' cuz they stay in the jar."

A client I appreciate much less than I do Diego follows. I find him too demanding, too old, and I feel as if he's giving me an unpleasant gynecological exam when I'm with him. He spends a good twenty minutes sitting on the bed, while I stand in front of him, his fat hairy fingers rummaging through my pussy. He tells me he'll be leaving for the

Bahamas in two weeks and surprises me by inviting me to come along, "You could spend your days on the beach while I'm attending meetings for work, we'd dine together in the evening and you could suck my dick each night." I picture myself with this month's edition of *Cosmopolitan* and the mandatory readings I must do for my university classes, lying down on a beach towel, my toes buried in the sand, a pen stuck between my lips, doing my homework while getting a tan. I refuse because I can't imagine spending a few hours next to him on the plane, because what he'd say about the Middle East conflict would disgust me too much, as would his fingers exploring my clit in between drinks served by business-class flight attendants.

A new client who's really cute with very short hair and his athletic body hidden underneath a light pink hipster[8] T-shirt does me on the kitchen counter. When he makes me climax, I feel like I'm about to faint, I'm quivering all over and trying to catch my breath. And when he orgasms inside me, he almost bursts into tears, and I can't stop staring at him, his dark eyes looking into mine, I'd like to keep him all day and fill all my thirty condom with his jizz. When he pulls out of me, he starts panicking, "The condom's still in you, I'm so sorry." I hop off the counter and go to the bathroom. "Fuck, fuck, fuck!" I take the condom out, washing my pussy for a good ten minutes while assuring him I'm disease free. As soon as he leaves, I feel like crying. I never felt at risk working at the agency, clients never stole money from me, and I never had to use the can of hairspray I keep under the bed to defend myself against men wanting to smash my head against a wall.

I call Stella, an organization located a block from where my cousin lives, offering support and free medical exams to sex workers. A girl tells me there's an STD screening center open every Monday evening. I try to convince myself the

8.  Very hip guy, a bit nerdy

client was too cute to be sick. I start praying the way I used to when I was fourteen before a mathematics exam, and go back to humming pop songs. I reapply my makeup and John, a New York State prison warden, consoles me. I'm always happy to see John. He's a shy mustachioed man who comes to Montreal to fuck me and see Quebec bands. Today, he offers me some dark chocolate, 70 per cent pure, and I don't know why but I feel like crying when I thank him. He turns down the light in the bedroom and tries to speak French to me while describing his house, "I'm repainting all the rooms, it'll take months, my house is huge, I'm painting them dove-gray." I ask him what color the walls used to be and he tells me they were already dove-gray, he repaints them every two years the same color. I give him a blow job and when he's on his way out, I realize I'm already feeling better and anxious to taste the chocolate he gave me before letting Samuel have the rest.

I figure out how much I owe Debbie and I barely finish reading the magazine *Loulou* another escort had left in the living room before my next client arrives. He tells me he moved to Quebec to find employment, but hasn't found any yet, so he spends his days working out at the YMCA and asks me if I can tell he's in good shape. He wants me to pretend I'm the girl he had asked to accompany him to his graduation and who had asked him to pop her cherry. I love role playing but Samuel never wants to play along with my fantasies. I'm happy to slow-dance with my client, I still remember a few tango and waltz steps I learned when I was in high school, and I undress, begging him to do me because I don't want to leave high school still a virgin. I tell him I dream of him every night, and I can see this is turning him on. He asks me to tell him about a fantasy of mine and I come up with a *Dawson's Creek* type story where a teenage boy who liked horror films fell in love with his best friend, a prudish girl always in plaid shirts. "Come over to my house, take a ladder, come up to my room. I'm pretending to be asleep and you touch me through my pajamas. I'm wearing unicorn-print pajamas and I'm holding a teddy bear in my arms. You stroke my pussy and you find it wet, and you penetrate me, sticking one of teddy's paws in my mouth so I won't wake my parents." My client ejaculates against my thigh. I can feel his hot and sticky sperm on my skin, and he kisses my mouth and promises he'll be back. "I wish I had met you when I was still a student. I was never very popular with girls. Would you have wanted to be my fuck friend?"

Nicky, an escort with 36D breasts, as pretty as a porn star, comes to take my place at 5 P.M. I wish her a pleasant evening, we chat for a few minutes, and I tell her about my last client. She smiles and says she has a regular client who likes to role play as well. "He takes two hours each week, on Friday nights, and wants me to pretend I'm a really mean cheerleader. I give him a spanking and throw him out in the corridor, stealing his glasses and threatening to smash them to pieces if he doesn't give me an immediate orgasm."

On my way home, with $600 in my gym bag, I stop at a convenience store and buy a *Star*, an *Us Weekly*, an *In Touch*, and some Skittles for Samuel. I used to buy celebrity gossip magazines only once a month, now I need my fix every week so I'll forget that I have nothing to say to my girlfriends and that I know nothing about them anymore. I'm really interested in what insults Lindsay Lohan wrote in a trendy New York bar bathroom aimed at Scarlett Johansson and I want to find out more about the fight between Jessica Simpson and Nick Lachey. I no longer speak to my friend Micha because I can't bear lying to her, and I think I'd disappoint her if I told her I was an escort. So, not to let her down, I prefer not seeing her anymore. That way she can't judge me. Even Samuel doesn't talk about it to his friends, though I gave him permission to tell his friend Julien, but I know what I do sometimes makes him uncomfortable, and he hates lying, it makes him nervous. But I believe he's afraid of what people might think, or maybe he's afraid his friends will tell him his mother was right, that I wasn't the right girl for him, too irresponsible, focusing too much on pleasure rather than making mac-and-cheese for her precious son.

I tell Samuel I want to stuff my face with fries and ketchup tonight, and he tells me he's up for it. He rolls a joint before asking me for some money to go to the deli around the corner. I give him a $20 bill and take this opportunity to surf the MERB Website and quickly go through all recent comments about me. "Nobody's perfect but I think Marissa's as close to perfection as can be. I'd love it if she could be my girlfriend!!!" and "I'll come see her whenever I can. The last thing she said to me was to dream of her while remembering our common passion." I couldn't have said that to a client, and I masturbate while waiting for Samuel, lying on my back on the red leather couch in the living room. When Samuel gets back, I tell him to fuck me before the fries get cold. I undo his pants and his limp dick surprises me, especially after I lick, kiss, and suck it. I lose my temper. "Fuck this, I screw all day and your cock still gets me wet but you don't want me? My clients get a hard-on as soon as I open the door, goddammit, and they're twenty years older than you." I leave him in the living room with all his fries and lock myself in our bedroom full of dirty bed sheets and broken blinds, with all our kittens and my favorite vibrator, and I climax, screaming very loudly, forgetting that our walls are paper-thin and that our neighbors can hear. I scream to upset him, so he'll react and open the door and slap me, saying he loves me despite the fact that I'm a whore, a stupid little whore he doesn't recognize anymore.

# Being Called a Slut vs. Finishing my Homework on Francis Ponge

I spend the afternoon on my balcony. It feels like summer already with that smelly self-tanning lotion on my face. I flip through a *Star* magazine that's comparing Lady Di's wedding ring to Camilla Parker Bowles' ring, who recently married Prince Charles. I look for a picture of Prince Harry, my favorite, just thinking about him makes me want to shove a dildo up my snatch, but I fight the urge. I don't want to touch myself before seeing clients tonight. I call my parents and ask them how Minus and Holden Caulfield are doing. They adopted two of Porcelaine's kittens, making my little brothers promise they'd care for them. My dad talks to me for a good twenty minutes on the phone and invites me to come have dinner at home with them the following Wednesday. I gladly accept, knowing I owe all my free time to the fact I'm an escort. I write down on my calendar that I have to go buy some cakes at the bakery next to my apartment or some maple-flavored chocolate at the Louise Décarie candy store, and buy a bottle of wine.

I down a sugar-free Guru and moan while slowly stretching, twisting my black locks around my fingers, hoping some passers-by walking on St. Denis Street will see me. I ready my gym bag and start looking for my white sequined blouse and the red skirt clients love because it makes my ass stick out. I wash the heels of my pumps, having worn them outside the other day to shop at Omer DeSerres for some brushes, canvases, and an easel. I leave a note for Samuel on our billboard. "Your brother called. Can you empty the litter box? I love you."

Outside the metro, a girl biting into a five-color Mr. Freeze makes me drool. When I turn onto Durocher Street by the Hilton Hotel, I debate if I should buy some ice cream at the convenience store. I bump into a client, a young Chinese man in love with me, who keeps trying to convince me to quit my job and be his wife. He promises me a luxurious apartment with my own private pool, telling me about all the jobs he applies for so he'll make more money and be able to pay for my tuition and all the dresses I could want. I pretend not to see him when I go into the light-orange-colored brick building. I call Debbie and ask her if Tin is my first client. She laughs knowing I can't stand his excessive fondness for me. "Yes, he called five hours ago, he wants to make sure he'll be your first tonight. He doesn't want to smell other clients on you. He'll stay for an hour and a half. Wait a bit in the hallway before knocking at Charline's door, she's still with someone."

I go see Brandon before checking if apartment 408 is free. He apologizes for the mess and takes me into his arms. I haven't seen him in a while. He tells me he's dating a girl who's completely crazy, a stripper who hit him last night while on crystal meth. "She's the only girl who doesn't complain when I do her for hours and she's gorgeous. We're going to go to Quebec City soon and getting tattooed together." He wishes me a good evening and invites me to come back and hang out in his apartment if I don't have too many clients. I add that I'm shocked, having found out that Pope John Paul II had passed away while touching myself in front of the TV.

Charline, a classical beauty resembling Ali MacGraw in

the movie *Love Story*, with her long brown hair parted in the middle and almond-shaped eyes, is out the door as soon as I arrive. She blows me a kiss, saying, "I have to go get my son at daycare." Before I have time to put on any makeup, Tin knocks impatiently. As I open the door he flicks his tongue in my mouth, a bouquet of roses behind his back. I'm so *not* a romantic, but I smile at Tin and ask him to give me a minute so I can put the roses into a glass of water. I already know I'm going to leave the roses in the apartment when I go home that night.

He tells me he brought a CD of one of his favorite musicians. I have to force myself not to laugh when I see it's a super (slang) kitsch Kenny G CD. "Sorry, Tin, we don't have any CD player here. I would have loved to get to know that artist." He's disappointed. "I wanted to massage you for an hour while you listened to Kenny G, to relax you."

He massages me, while talking about the car he just bought. "My parents are very proud of me. In China, automobiles are too expensive." Which reminds me I have to buy some indoor plants and a ceramic pot at Farfelu, a home décor boutique, and schedule an appointment for a tanning session at Spa Diva, Tony Soprano's lookalike compliments me when I'm not as pale as Dita Von Teese. I can't relax. I don't like my client's thin fingers or the oil he rubs me with, so I pretend to fall asleep to make him happy and so he'll shut up about cars. When he asks me to give him a body rub, I get up and wash myself in the bathroom before the oil permeates my skin and makes me smell like a lavender field for my next clients. Tin joins me in the bathroom, takes my hand, and offers to wash me. I refuse saying I'll be back in the bedroom in a jiffy. He stops cold. "You know I love you. Why do you do this? Why don't you want me to be your man? Do you have to do this? Do you owe people money?" I get irritated. "I work here because I like it. I told you already." He says he hopes I'll change my mind. When I tell him I won't, he puts his hands over his eyes and starts screaming. I leave the bathroom, closing the door behind me, take my money, and ask Brandon to get rid of Tin before the neighbors complain about the noise.

I get back to the apartment fifteen minutes later and Debbie assures me over the phone I'll never have Tin as a client again. She apologizes and says Brandon, she, and I should have dinner soon. She says a New York woman will come see me sometime this evening. My first thought is I'm going to have a lady client and I start worrying, unsure if I'm good enough to find her G-spot, but Debbie says she might want to join the agency. I'm to talk to her about the work and see if the girl's ready to get screwed for eight hours straight, several times a week. Proud that Debbie trusts me, I practice my hard-to-get look in the mirror.

A Los Angeles cameraman in Montreal for about ten days or so books thirty minutes with me. Though curious, I refrain from asking him which movie he's working on. An English-speaking businessman follows him, complaining about his wife. I hate all my clients' wives, thinking they're unfair for not wanting to suck their husbands' dicks after a hard day's work, and finding them ridiculous for spending the day with girlfriends getting manicures instead of staying at home, ironing their husbands' shirts. I swear to myself that I'll try to be nicer, that I'll never say no to sex even if I have a headache, and that I'll continue buying sexy lingerie, and he abruptly penetrates me. "Tell me you like being my little bitch." I scream with delight, "I like being your little bitch." He pulls my hair. "You're my whore." I manage to look at him out of the corner of my eye and stick my tongue out at him before he shoves my face into a pillow. I love him for daring to insult me and taking me violently, so I add, "I love it when you fuck my cunt, I love being your bitch, I deserve to be fucked real hard by your cock." He comes, his red face against mine, and pulls my hair really hard. I thank him. Still lying on top of me he says, "You like it for real. That's what excites me the most." He lets on that he often pays for escorts and transsexuals, but never sees the same one twice. "Maybe for you, I'll make an exception. You're a good little bitch." I get him an ashtray so he can smoke a cigarette in bed, dripping with sweat.

Debbie informs me the New York girl's on her way and I have an hour before my next client. A frail girl comes into the apartment. She's skinnier than I am. I don't find her attractive with her hair wet from the rain. We introduce ourselves, she tells me she has a B.A. in Art History and has been working as an escort in New York City, where she doesn't sleep with her clients, only going out on the town with them. I tell her the agency rates and she's surprised. She used to make twice that in NYC without having to take her clothes off. She still feels like trying, so I call Debbie in front of her, tell my her the girl's measurements, and suggest we see a client together, which delights Debbie.

Our client is the athletic hipster who had scared me so much by leaving a condom full of cum inside me. I introduce him to Estelle and tell him for only $100 more he could do us both. The idea of being with a beginner turns him on. He tells me his first name's Alex. I drag him to the living room and tell him I find him really sexy and not to worry, "I got tested. I'm clean." He says he trusts me, while getting down on his knees, lowering my skirt, and pushing my panties aside. He starts licking my cunt. I play with his hair. I feel like leaving Estelle aside but I call to her, "Alex's eating my pussy out! Come taste me too!" She appears in the doorway, wearing pelican-print undies. I motion her to approach and she kisses me on the mouth. Alex sits me down on the living room table and lowers his pants. I put him in my mouth while Estelle plays with his balls. I push them both away then take them to the bedroom. Alex stops me and makes me sit down on the hallway floor, spreading my legs while Estelle licks me, her little ass raised. I look at Alex admiring her ass, swallowing with difficulty, and watch him spread Estelle's legs and fuck her while staring at me. Alex comes in no time, telling me right after that he'd like to see me outside of work, to fuck me longer. I give him my phone number without thinking about it, mesmerized by him. I smell his sperm inside the condom before throwing it into the kitchen trashcan. I bid farewell to Estelle, telling her I hope to see her again soon. She's not as pretty as Cindy or Charline but she sure knows how to use her tongue around my clit. I'll definitely be thinking about her the rest of the evening.

A thirty-something McGill University literature professor doesn't believe me when I say I love Shakespeare as much as he does while we're fucking and spooning. Panting, I recite a passage of *Hamlet*, and that impresses him because his students, thanks to Leonardo DiCaprio, only know *Romeo & Juliet*. Before heading home, I also have sex with a lawyer who was just hired by a firm, in dire need of a blow job to make him feel better. "I'm positive my bosses won't like me. Law's not for me. But I like how you suck my dick. Tell me I'll win a case soon, Marissa."

The next day, I get up at 10 A.M. and jog for an hour. I try to convince Samuel to join me because I think he could lose a good fifteen pounds, but he prefers staying at home, preparing spaghetti sauce to offer the neighbors. I go to Archambault and buy my mother *By a Slow River*, Carmen Electra's exercise video *Aerobic Striptease*, and some cherry stem herbal tea. I walk home from the grocery store with six plastic bags, full of jars of Nutella, cinnamon buns, smoked salmon, light salad dressing, lemon-flavored and pink grapefruit-flavored water, all knocking against my legs. I'm sure this will leave bruises. I wake Samuel when I get back, discouraged to see him like this, still hidden under the blankets as if he could sleep fifteen consecutive hours when I force myself to work twenty-five hours a week, getting poked and probed by men, running and sweating the rest of the time so everyone will see how extraordinarily thin, healthy, and pretty I am.

I give Samuel the sweater I want him to wear at my parents' dinner. It's made of striped gray and forest green wool. He doesn't ask me why and puts it on before brushing his teeth and fixing himself some scrambled eggs and beans in tomato sauce. I feel so distant from him, so close to crying and telling him I stopped loving him because he didn't want to go running with me this morning. Feeling as if I'm the only one striving to be more than adorable exhausts me. I don't need Samuel, I don't need anyone anymore, I can only rely on my body, willing to arch itself, open itself, fit into extra small outfits, give itself to clients, my pussy always soft, my legs tanned and golden, marked by my tight thigh-high stockings, my body stronger than I suspected it could be, never once catching a cold even during the winter months, despite kissing all my clients.

I congratulate my parents on their new living room décor and run around looking for Minus and Holden Caulfield, while keeping an ear out for what Samuel says, ready to interrupt him at any moment if he says something inappropriate. I weigh myself before and after the meal, taking my dress off. I'm proud of myself, despite my father having held me by the arm saying I'm too thin in a worried almost scared tone when I refused to have a bite of the almond cake I had brought. My mom asks me what exercises I do to have such thin and muscular thighs, and I don't tell her spending hours sitting on a guy can do wonders.

Samuel and I leave early. I have to write a ten-page essay on Francis Ponge. I start to panic as soon as we reach the apartment. I sprawl on the wooden floor and ask Samuel to lie on top of me. When he refuses I scream and crawl to Porcelaine and curl up in a ball next to her, crying, telling Samuel he can't understand. "I shouldn't have to do homework, only fuck and forget everything else, drop out of school, leave you, and you could keep our stupid TV that's just too big. I'm tired Samuel, so tired, and you do nothing." He holds me in his arms and cries. I push him away, hating to hear him cry, then ask for his forgiveness, putting my head down on his thighs, promising him all will be fine. I get up to go wash my face and stare at myself in the mirror and find my puffed up eyes, my bitten lips, and my long messy black hair pretty. I continue crying silently in front of the mirror while telling myself life would be much easier without having to love Samuel, only caring for clients a couple of hours a day.

Samuel writes half my Francis Ponge paper, and I drop it off late without even showing up to class, sliding it in the literature department's mailbox. I feel free. I know I'll have a great summer, and I show up at the Maisonneuve College where Fabrice teaches and wait for him in front of his office. When he gets there we go to Boudoir where I sip a pale ale for an hour. He says he wants to fuck me. I uneasily refuse, "I need to work at the agency tomorrow and I don't want to be sore. Do you want me to blow you instead?" We walk to Lafontaine Park, a big Montreal park with a pond full of ducks and policemen doing rounds every so often to make sure no one's fucking in the bushes or behind a tree. We come to the park's lodge, not a very discreet shelter, but I don't care. I lower Fabrice's jeans and find him already hard. I lick the tip of his penis. He asks me if I've ever had affairs with other professors. I shake my head and drive his cock deep in my throat. I jerk him off and he quickly orgasms. Wiping my mouth with my hand, I wonder, "What about you, has any other student blown you in your office instead of going to eat lunch at the cafeteria?"

He takes me home, where I apply St. Ives' Collagen Elastin hydrating lotion all over my body, by the light of a raspberry-scented candle. I go to bed, kiss Samuel holding a stuffed tiger in my arms. I wake up at noon, do some aerobics in front of the TV when I get a call from Alex while Samuel is at the neighbors offering them homemade spaghetti sauce. Alex saw on the agency's Website that I was scheduled to work tonight. He proposes I visit him first at his photography studio. I write down the directions, looking forward to seeing his loft among the Greek restaurants and next to the Oh La La store on the very lively St. Laurent Street. I look through my closet and opt for a denim skirt, a white shirt, and a gemstone necklace bought at the Miss Swiss store with my mother. I almost never wear necklaces to work to prevent clients from strangling me with them.

I walk through St. Louis Square and find Alex's loft. He greets me by asking if he can give me less than he pays me at the agency and gives me $125. I'm impressed by his studio, high ceilings with white walls full of travel shots and pictures of girls in New York City bar bathrooms. There's a black leather armchair and a mattress on the floor. "I lived here a few months when I hadn't found an apartment. But I couldn't sleep, it was too noisy with the street traffic and the guy upstairs who's into S&M or satanic rituals, I'm not sure, but I could hear him screaming and on the other side of the street there's an insurance broker who killed himself. The walls were covered in blood, the elevator smelled of incense as usual, but upstairs it was horrible with the stench of putrefaction." He raises my arms and lifts my cami over my head. He vigorously fucks me doggy-style and each pelvic thrust gets me close to orgasm. He's so good, I want to tell him he's the best client in the whole wide world, but he wouldn't believe me, so I only moan like a good little bitch until I hear him whine, while sending a big squirt of cum in an extra-large condom, "No, no, no. Not yet." I feel like laughing when he collapses on top of me. We talk about his photos, about the *Sin City* movie, and about *Hustler,* and I leave him warning Debbie I'll be a bit late.

I stop at a Coffee Depot and order green tea. I hop into a cab, the back of my neck and hair still smelling of his cologne.

# Like a Jungle Book She-Wolf During the Formula 1 Grand Prix

I'm always a bit embarrassed going to the bank, my hair tied up in two ponytails with little pink ribbons and $5,000 in my Franco Sarto handbag. When I give the money to the teller, I'm not watching her count the bills, but rather I'm wondering what she thinks of me, can she tell I'm an escort, or does she think I'm a dope dealer's girlfriend. The teller informs me of the exact amount I'm depositing, I sign a receipt, and exit on Mont-Royal Street. It's hot outside. I am wearing a yellow and blue flowery blouse, and have the whole day in front of me. I feel like buying some glasses with princesses painted on them at Farfelu, some cotton dresses at American Apparel, and some books I can read later on my balcony or sitting in the grass by the metro station.

I stop at the Bouquinerie du Plateau,[9] looking for a comic book for Samuel, so I head towards the children's section and find a Christophe Honoré book, *Mon cœur bouleversé*, a lucky find. I love Marcel and his big brother Léo's adventures, but reading the first lines of the book I realize Léo died of AIDS. This brings tears to my eyes. I hold on to the book while I look for a lighter one but come across

---

9. A secondhand bookseller in the hip Montreal neighborhood called the Plateau.

another children's book about a redhead kid with AIDS. I silently pray, "I never ever want to get sick, I shouldn't have slept with that scrawny client, I shouldn't have kissed him, but it's true you need about five pounds of saliva to catch this and I didn't kiss him that long, please God, I swear I'll start saving some money to donate to associations if my next test is negative...I also swear I'll buy fewer shoes. And stop badmouthing people who try to get signatures for Greenpeace petitions, and call my grandmother more often even though talking to her hurts my ears." I buy the books, purchase some sugar-free Red Bull, Perrier mineral water, honey-roasted almonds, and green apples. My tummy hurts and I can't wait to get back home to lie down until the pain goes away.

My pain goes away quickly. I swallow some zinc and vitamin C tablets. I change into a psychedelic print bikini *à la* Austin Powers. I look at my small ass, making sure I'm cellulite-free, and apply some self-tanning lotion all over my body. I wait for it to penetrate my skin, sucking on a Coca Cola-flavored lollipop, and lie down on a La Vie en Rose[10] beach towel with Porcelaine. I read an excerpt from a Yeats poem on the cover of one of the books I bought at the Bouquinerie du Plateau:

> For love is but a skein unwound
> Between the dark and dawn
> A lonely ghost the ghost is
> That to God shall come

I close my eyes, my head resting on my forearm for a moment before thinking about strange tan lines.

I wait for Samuel's return. I feel like going for a sangria at La Petite Marche. When he arrives, he says I stink. I pretend to slap him. "It's not my fault, it's the tanning lotion. And

10. Canadian lingerie retail store chain

I can't shower right away." I douse myself in Givenchy's Very Irresistible, throw my bikini on the hallway floor and proceed, holding onto Samuel's arm, towards the Franco-Italian bistro right in front of the National Theatre School, two minutes from our apartment. I take a few free weekly newspapers and look at the escort agencies' ads with lots of girls dressed up as sexy Formula 1 drivers. I feel anxious, the weekend of June 12 and 13 will be very busy with thousands of tourists coming to Montreal to party because of the races and the fashion shows happening at the same time. I don't want to get a yeast infection because of all the big dicks rubbing against my cunt in under-lubricated condoms. We slowly drink our sangria, and I eat the blueberries and strawberries at the bottom of the pitcher with a spoon. We talk to some literature students and I ask Samuel if he wants to come with me to the Théâtre d'aujourd'hui next week to see the play *La condition triviale*.[11] A friend of mine wrote it, it's about a girl who embroiders silk hearts inside her husband's coat pockets, while he fucks a female stranger he met on the street.

I leave a $10 tip for the blonde waitress and Samuel, pointing to the Crémerie Meu Meu, feels like having a soft ice cream cone. We jaywalk across the street and I wait for him on a street bench, gazing into closed clothing store windows. I force myself to rest my head on Samuel's shoulder, trying to prove to him I didn't turn into a frigid bitch unable to tolerate his presence across a restaurant table.

On the eve of the Montreal Grand Prix, I start work at 5 P.M., arriving at the agency in a white bohemian skirt, pink flip-flops, a tight cami, and no bra. I change into a super tight black Marciano dress and apply eyeliner. In the medicine cabinet, I find a lightening cream for mixed skins, and I wonder what escort it belongs to, and some Juicy Fruit

---

11. Literally, *The Mundane Condition*

gum. I chew some gum and watch a rerun of *Les Francs-tireurs*,[12] with Amir Khadir's[13] take on Islam.

A new client arrives. He's handsome and very well dressed, and offers me a lemon-flavored alcoholic beverage, but I politely decline, "You can have some while I take care of you but I can't drink any, it puts me to sleep." He tells me he did a little bit of blow before coming to see me and he only wants to talk to me. "How long have you been an escort? I'm from Switzerland, but I just bought a condo in Old Montreal, you can come visit me, I always have coke handy, but my dick is limp because of it, I'm a lawyer and haven't been in Quebec long, I don't know anyone, Swiss whores are strangers to me, I used to be a gigolo for a forty-year-old woman, she took me to Portugal for a weekend and gave me $4,000 or $5,000." I encourage him to undress in the kitchen. He puts his clothes in a pile on the counter, and I notice some toilet paper stuck between his ass cheeks, which I find disgusting, but I know Debbie will die laughing when I tell her.

The Swiss man writes his phone number in my Paperblanks notebook and leaves, letting Binh-Binh in, proudly wearing a Ferrari cap on his head. He informs me he also has a Ferrari polo shirt and so does his cousin, and they'll dress alike to watch the Grand Prix. I feign being impressed, but I never liked cars and never had any Jacques Villeneuve[14] posters on my bedroom walls even when he

---

12. Literally, *The Straight Shooters*. A French-language Quebec TV socio-cultural magazine specializing in in-depth interviews with local and international political and cultural personalities.

13. Amir Khadir is a left-wing Quebec politician born in Iran, spokesperson for the Québec Solidaire party.

14. French-Canadian automobile racing driver, son of driver Gilles Villeneuve, idolized for how he looks as for much as his driving performances.

had bleached hair and enough groupies to hear his Monaco accent on all the national TV stations.

An hour goes by before my next client. I'm telling myself Debbie probably didn't spend as much in advertising as the other ten main agencies. I'm a bit disappointed. I thought it was the time of year when escorts made the most money. I was getting ready to buy plane tickets to Italy the next day, thinking I was going to make $5,000 over the weekend. A sport photographer, known for his volleyball championship photos, tells me he can't stay long because he has dinner reservations at Chez Alexandre, a downtown restaurant on Peel Street renowned for its depraved preppy clientele as well as its gorgeous waitresses in short black miniskirts. He shows me the medical certificate he had promised to give me last time when I refused to swallow his sperm. "God! You really want me to taste you if you went to see a doctor just for me..." He tells me, half-panting, that he sees one twice a year, to satisfy his insurance company because he travels the world. I stroke his torso and lower his pants. I strive to give him an amazing fellatio and I swallow every drop. I wish him a pleasant evening and he gives me a $60 tip.

Debbie calls to ask me if I mind going out. An American client, a regular at the agency, is in a downtown hotel willing to pay more for someone to go to him. I get changed, not wanting the taxi driver or the hotel doorman to know I'm a call girl, but I giggle wondering what the client will think of my bohemian skirt. I hail a cab on Sherbrooke Street and it's mayhem. We're stuck in traffic for twenty minutes because of the Grand Prix festivities. I get out, ready to walk when I realize I forgot to bring condoms with me. Hating myself, I call Debbie so she can warn the client I'll be late. I stop at a convenience store and ask the cashier for some condoms. He gives me two, cherry-flavored. I arrive at the hotel and no one asks me any questions, I must look like a tourist with my sandals. In the elevator I check if my hair's okay, if my armpits smell, or if I forgot to remove any unwanted hair on my upper lip. The client seems unfazed by my tardiness and pays me for the whole hour despite the fact I'll need to leave in thirty minutes because he needs to go meet friends at the casino. He smells like a hamburger. I kiss him and position myself on all fours on his king-size bed, facing a mirror. He puts his hands on my hips and does quick movements, his balls hitting my pussy and I climax before him, howling like a she-wolf from the *Jungle Book.*

Back at apartment 408, I take a lukewarm shower and turn on the air conditioning and fan in the bedroom. I'm shocked to find only two clean towels and I apologize for my wet hair to the next client, a thirty-something seven-foot-tall giant with a shaved head. He wants to stay with me for thirty minutes. He winks and heads to the bedroom, "You want to put your slutty lips on my big dick?" He takes his pants off and smiles when I realize his cock's not big, it's huge, as large as eight Asian dicks or two black cocks and as long as three Chupa Chups lollipops.

I'm afraid he'll break me and I'll never be able to fuck again if I sit on his dick, so I'm very relieved to hear he wants me only to blow him, though I have no idea how I'll ever be able to open my mouth wide enough to let his prick touch the roof of my mouth. I can't even put a condom on his schlong, I don't have any his size. I give small licks to the tip of his penis, when I open my mouth I can feel my teeth against his skin. But he doesn't complain, "You're doing great, I'll tell you when I'm about to climax so you can see my cum squirt, that'll turn you on, bitch." I'm sure I have a major jaw cramp, when he takes me in his arms and kisses my forehead. He gives me a generous $80 tip; I can't help but secretly hope never to see him again just in case he feels like fucking my twat next time.

Colin, the comic book artist who freelances for advertising

agencies, is my next client. Just the thought of him tires me. I know he'll tell me at least thirty times he loves me. He gently gives me a white bank envelope. I don't count it, already knowing there's $420 in it. He takes two hours once a week, or one hour when he's sure to come back later in the week. He tells me he brought his drawing board and would like to draw me, fully clothed. "You remind me of Jennifer Connelly. I like your green eyes. You'll inspire me to draw a superhero." I laugh, "No comic book hero has small breasts!" He also takes out of his bag a Tupperware container full of celery sticks and carrots, which he shares with me. I thank him, taking some celery, but the mere thought of eating while I'm working at the agency makes me queasy. I ask him to position me, I don't know how to pose for him. He sits me down on the bed, my ass on a pillow, my back against a wall. While he draws me, I talk about Charles Bukowski, psychoanalysis, and mispronounce Carl Jung's name. He likes correcting me and teasing me. I tell him about my cats and Porcelaine's new habit of sleeping on my back, not counting the fact she likes taking baths with me. He says he'll probably buy a bird soon, he misses his albino parakeet. He forces me to eat some carrots and celery sticks then leaves with some pre-cum on his pants.

I then head over to Alex's, his address and phone number written on the palm of my hand. Last time I saw him, he took me out to a Greek restaurant and my dress was crumpled because we had fucked an hour before while fully dressed and then had eaten some cherries, spitting the pits on his St. Laurent Street loft's floor. When he opens the door, he hugs me saying, "We wait, okay, let's not fuck right away." Five minutes later I'm in his bed, straddling him, he's rubbing against me, and I feel him getting a hard-on. He takes off my black wool sweater, "You must be hot." I take off my bra and lean over him so he can kiss my breasts. He flips me over, teasing my anus, I raise my ass, inviting him to penetrate my cunt right away, and while we're fucking I notice on his bed stand a book to improve his vocabulary. He brings me back on top of him, I put my feet on his shoulders, trying not to look at a painting hung over his bed of a big orange fish next to the Eiffel Tower, and I run my fingers through his dark hair, already full of sweat. His urgency to fuck me and make me climax turns me on. I can feel my juice dripping over his balls.

I take the tissue he used to take off his condom and throw it into the bathroom trash can. On the back of the toilet is a magazine full of girls in bathing suits. I go through it, I like their long curly hair and their rock-hard tits. I rummage through his cabinets, find some menstrual pads and necklaces, and recall his girlfriend left him two or three weeks ago. I don't remember what he told me about it, but I find it sad to see what's left of her in his apartment. When I emerge from the bathroom, he's in the kitchen asking me if I like almonds before adding a ton to the salad. I ask if I can help him, just to be polite, despite being scared stiff of his calling my bluff. I can't cook for shit. He gives me a cucumber to slice and I apply myself as if the whole evening depended on the size of the slices. He comes behind me, forcing me to bend over. I put my face on the counter, next to the knife, and he bites my neck, calling me by my real name, "Mélodie, you look famished."

Before heading outside to eat on a metallic table, I ask him about the child portrait glued to his window. He smiles and says it's his nephew who lives on Mauritius Island. He asks me if I want to have kids and I nod, my eyes full of tears. I should start saving up for a stroller, stuffed animals, and disposable diapers before I stop working as an escort. He tells me he does also, "I'm thirty-nine. I'd like to be a father before the age of forty-five." I'm surprised at how old he is, I thought he was around thirty. Stroking my cheek, he adds, "I eat healthy, I bike around the city, and I play soccer. Sometimes in the park, I end up alone with another guy my age. After school, kids now prefer going home to play videogames." We talk about our hopes and dreams and he informs me he might not make any profit this year with his photography studio and I change the subject. Money talk always makes me uncomfortable.

We head back inside to watch the movie *Or (My Treasure)*, a Franco-Israeli film with actresses pretending to be prostitutes in the Holy Land. I don't feel like reading subtitles and Alex falls asleep on my lap. I wonder if I should go, or stroke his back, or his hair, or gently push him away. I read the bills on the living room table. Some are under Alex's ex-girlfriend's name. I hear my cell phone ringing and ignore it, but it rings again ten minutes later and I figure it must be Samuel worrying about me. I wake up Alex and head back home, thanking him for the evening and promising I'll come hang out with him again next week.

On Friday morning, I bring the new *Us Weekly* with me to the agency. Jessica Simpson is on the cover as Daisy Duke. Along with her personal stylist Rachel Zoe, whom I hear encourages anorexia among all the Hollywood starlets. I entertain a seventy-year-old client. I've never been with anyone that old. His almost translucent skin, his big blue veins, and his liver spots all over his body move me. I don't mind his flabby ass. I'm touched, despite being afraid of getting old. I'll probably have to get Botox injections when I turn twenty-seven, and I find almost all the men I fuck handsome, be they twenty-five or seventy, and if they wear shirts adorned by cuff-links even better.

I get a new client next. I know I'm getting them because of all the comments people leave about me on MERB, but I miss my regulars. I want to know if Tony Soprano's still at war with his wife who's asking him to raise his life insurance premium to match those of her rich new TMR[15] gold digger

___
15. Town of Mount Royal, a rich Anglo town just northwest of downtown Montreal

friends' husbands. I'd like to hear the young lawyer tell me he won his first jury case, or not. This client hesitates between spending a half hour or a full hour with me, and finally opts for an hour, which I tell Debbie. He pays me and we head to the bedroom. I sit next to him, putting my hand on his thigh, and he curses while removing my hand. "Can I change it to just a half hour?" He had ejaculated. I feel bad. I sometimes get clients who can't come but this is the first time I'm with a guy who climaxes in ten seconds just because I put my hand on his lap. I can't reimburse him. Debbie doesn't allow it. "I can't give you your money back but it's okay, I can give you a massage and we can fuck later..." He's either too embarrassed or mad, but he finally leaves after locking himself in the bathroom for ten minutes.

Brandon lets me know I have to go get clean sheets in the basement laundry room. I go down without bumping into anyone, and start folding the striped bed sheets when Daniel, a client of mine who takes care of his bedridden grandmother, arrives. He's always so nice, and his British accent is so adorable. He forces himself to speak French with me but for the last month he's been feeling comfortable enough with me to become, without prior notice, a brute between the sheets. When I start blowing him, he holds my head down, so I can't breathe. He knows I wouldn't let anyone else do this to me, but I like it with him. He pulls my hair. I stand up straight. He loses his nice Anglo smile and slaps me. I try not to react, continue gazing into his eyes, and he pushes me towards his dick. I take the condom off and he ejaculates on my face. I close my eyes and he gently takes a tissue to wipe my skin. I take a shower before he leaves and we talk as if he hadn't slapped me. He tells me some cousins from New York City will come visit him for two weeks and he bought some football tickets.

I have time to nap while watching two *Gilmore Girls* episodes on the French-language channel VRAK-TV, refuse to see a client who wanted to swap an orgasm for a condomless blow job, write in my Paperblanks notebook that I want to buy a military vest at Le Château and a M.A.C. eyebrow pencil, and receive a thousand thanks from a small-dicked client I fucked while sitting on top, my back turned to him, before 5 P.M. I'm getting ready to leave when Debbie begs me to stay, the escort taking my place is late and there's a client waiting. I reapply some makeup and the client tells me in a rude tone that he'll stay an hour. I say no, he can take thirty minutes, and he gets furious, "My imam gave me an exemption. I want to take advantage of it for an hour. I want to do it all for a whole hour." I tell him he can wait for the next girl to arrive, or stay with me but for only half an hour. He finally accepts, but because he's furious he doesn't get hard, making him even more furious. I pretend not to hear him and I lick his balls. He asks me to put my finger up his ass and I refuse. He persists, "I'm clean." I continue licking his balls until he gets a hard-on, and I take the opportunity quickly to put a condom on his dick, successfully, spitting on it before blowing him. He throws me on the floor, on my back, and takes me like this while violently kissing me.

A new escort, a super cheerful Asian girl with acne stands in for me when I leave and I ask Samuel to meet me at the McDonald's by the UQAM.[16] I have an urge to devour a cheeseburger and salty fries. I bump into a high school friend on the metro. I talk to her for only two minutes, laughing too loudly and hugging her too tightly, telling her I just finished working at a daycare center and I'm off to meet Samuel, saying her necklace is too cute while almost running away from her, quite nervous.

---

16. University of Quebec in Montreal

# Things One Should Never Say to a Client

1. "The client before you lost his condom in my pussy."

2. "Oh. My. God. Your dick is huge."
(...if his cock's one inch long when he's hard. He may have a small member but he's not stupid.)

3. "I became an escort to buy my three kids' whole wheat pasta, my husband's blow, and to pay for my mother's chemotherapy."

4. "I'm an escort in order to be able to write a bestseller in two years. I'll talk about you and what color shirts you wear, how you moan when you climax, and what you'll never tell your second wife."

5. "Tomorrow's my third wedding anniversary."
(Some clients may get turned on by a whore who has a boyfriend but usually it annoys them. It ruins the image that he's the most important guy in the whore's pussy and mind.)

6. "Wearing a condom is mandatory if you don't want to catch herpes or gonorrhea from me."

7. "I'm wearing some Dior perfume mixed with the previous client's sperm. I didn't have enough time to wash."

8. "I wear a long blonde wig to hide the fact I'm a green-haired anarchist with the same haircut as your favorite hockey player."

9. "You can't put your hand on my head when I'm blowing you because it reminds me of my stepfather, my uncle, and my neighbor forcing me to do that every Saturday morning in front of Stop the Smoggies."

10. "Have you ever had sex with a girl without having to pay for it?"

# At the Amusement Park or in a Motel Room All I Think About Are Sexy Daddies

On a sunny morning, my legs covered in bruises from carrying home grocery bags full of green apples, water bottles, spinach pizza, and smoked salmon, I put on pink Old Navy short shorts and a Care Bears T-shirt and tell Samuel to get his backpack. We hail a taxi and head for La Ronde, an amusement park on St. Helen's Island, twenty minutes from our apartment. I'm excited, despite having to stand in line behind loads of teenage girls to get tickets. I haven't been to an amusement park since I was sixteen. I stretch while I wait to pay, not caring what others might think. I owe my ballerina legs to spending all my time dancing *en pointe*.

Samuel wins a plush duck that I baptize Grandfather Henry while pouring some water over it. I read the graffiti written inside the rides and ask Samuel to take a picture of me making a really scared face on the pirate boat ride, as they do in the *Stars – They're Just Like Us* section of an American gossip magazine. I buy some pink cotton candy that I eat while watching a little girl kick another one, in the lineup to ride the oldest merry-go-round in North America. I feel so happy. I'd love to spend all my days in amusement parks, trying to win the biggest stuffed animals, drooling over caramel-flavored ice cream, and screaming at the top of my lungs on roller-coasters, surrounded by daddies who must see escorts from time to time and teenagers in tank tops and even shinier lip gloss than mine.

We leave at closing time, tanned and five years younger. At home I wait for Samuel to hop into the shower. I don't want to needlessly hurt him. I grab Gontran, my darling rat, put him on my shoulder, and surf the MERB Website. A new comment has been added about me: "More than a month ago, I spent half an hour with Marissa. Her attitude and professionalism impressed me. She's great at what she does. The only problem is that she's very skinny. I'm a tall man and I like big white girls with big boobs. Nonetheless, I'd say it was worth it. I had read many positive comments about her and I had wanted to see for myself. She's amazing and really wants to please you. She did an excellent job licking my balls, nipples, belly, and the inside of my thighs." Very proud of myself, I give Gontran a radish and join Samuel in the shower. I get him hard by sucking his cock. He turns the water off, we step out of the shower, and he does me on the bathroom counter, banging my head against the mirror.

I feel tired when I go back to the agency. I didn't sleep well, God knows why. I was too hot, kept thinking about having to pick my next semester's courses and about the gift I'll have to buy my parents for their twentieth wedding anniversary. I hope I won't be too busy today. I can't wait to be with Samuel after he returns from visiting his mother whom I don't like in Repentigny. She calls me irresponsible and sees me as a little princess, when at the same time she flies to the Dominican Republic, courtesy of her lover, and drinks every night while talking nonstop about her garden. I avoid seeing her as much as I can, although I know it saddens Samuel, but I don't like rubbing shoulders with people who make me unhappy. I always want to feel special and she reflects an image of me I can't stand, the one of a little girl who'll never be good enough for her and who doesn't read enough Danielle Steel novels.

An American psychiatrist on holiday does me doggy-style. He leaves me, checking if his shirt still smells of my perfume, saying "I could die here and be happy."

A construction site foreman offers to go down on me while sucking on a Halls mint lozenge, but doesn't have enough money to afford that extra. He's dripping with sweat after having fucked me and the sheets are so wet I have to change them before entertaining a black man who ejaculates on my breasts. I thank God he hadn't wanted to penetrate me, he had such a huge dick. I feel as if I'm getting a yeast infection. I feel dry, hypersensitive, and my insides seem to have been ripped open. I need a vacation. I'm too popular these days. Clients stay with me for a long time, talking about their favorite radio shows, rock-climbing, or their kids playing on soccer or baseball teams. I want to spend a week in California, maybe in Orange County where the characters of my favorite show live, or go to Spain.

Colin comes to see me, saying he won't touch me, he doesn't want to objectify me. I'm not sure how to react. I don't mind being thought of as a doll, I find it easier opening my legs than my mouth, not that I have anything against Colin. He wants me to tell him about my family. He has a sister who wishes good night to her four bedroom walls and says *amen* to her door frame before going to sleep. He wants to know how many men asked me to marry them since I began working for the agency. I giggle and apologize for the construction noise next door.

I'm very surprised to see Alex next. Calling me Marissa instead of Mélodie, he gives me the last $10 he owes me in Loonies[17] and quarters. He kisses me fiercely, his teeth hitting mine. "I'm disappointed. You didn't call me. I don't want you ever to do that again." I tell him I didn't have time

---

17. Canadian 1-dollar coin

to go see him, but he disturbs me, and I vow never to see him again after our hour's up. He asks me to promise him I'll never do that again. "I need you, I thought you loved me, I want you so much, you're so beautiful, so gorgeous, say you're only mine." I'm starting to feel that he wants me too much, but I tell him what he wants to hear, that I dressed up for his eyes only and was waiting for him, "Each time a man knocks at the door, I hope it's you." He wants me on top. I would have preferred it doggy-style, that way I wouldn't have to look at him.

Debbie tells me I can leave early if I wish, since there's no other client and she won't be able to answer the calls as she has some shopping to do. I thank her and meet Samuel at Crèmerie Pineault. He orders a pear-flavored soft ice cream cone and I opt for a banana and strawberry sherbet. I leave it unfinished on the outside table, thinking pigeons will feast on it. I tell him I'd like to stop by a travel agency, so we can go away together for at least a week, maybe to California, see the place that launched Jim Morrison's career, one of his idols.

Back at the apartment, I can't stop looking at the time, unable to sleep, listening to music until neighbors start banging on the wall. I ask Samuel to give me head, incapable of climaxing by myself. I leave the lights off, imagining it's Carmen Electra instead of my boyfriend sucking on my clit. I can't focus on my pleasure. "I'd like to adopt a porcupine from a Montreal farm." He goes down on me for almost an hour, his goatee tickling me. I arch my back, sticking my pussy in his face. He tells me I got so wet I've created a pond on the bed sheets. I kiss him and bid him sweet dreams, quite calm now.

In Dorval, I stop at a mall and buy some egg sandwiches and lubricant, and watch Musique Plus for half an hour at the motel while checking through the peephole every time

I hear a noise. A future male nurse studying at Dawson College is celebrating his thirtieth birthday. He has sparse white hairs in his goatee, he fucks me saying he'll make me climax as I've never climaxed before, "I'm not good, I'm better than good." I pretend I'm in ecstasy after fifteen minutes because it's his birthday, and he inserts a finger in my pussy to feel his big hard dick in my twat. A lawyer who visits me once a month, wearing a lemon-print shirt, asks me to suck his nipples really hard and he fucks me, my belly flat on the dirty comforter. He takes the condom afterwards and swallows his cum, telling me in a very important voice, "I want you to fall in love with me."

My landlord calls me. He says the alarm system I had installed is malfunctioning, and there have been complaints from the neighbors. It's been ringing for the last hour. I apologize and tell him I can't leave now. I hope my cats won't be too terrorized.

Pierre arrives, all smiles, with his glass bottle of green tea, which he's been drinking nonstop now that he's in remission from two cancers. He's a giant from Texas who comes to Montreal once or twice a month to indulge in a weekend of debauchery. He sees escorts, has fun in strip joints, sometimes with Brandon, and says his doctors find him healthier than ever after a trip to Montreal. "Sex is the cure. You should advertise this, Marissa. I'm alive 'cause of you, my little sweetie." He bursts into laughter. I love him. I've never met anyone happier. He lets me touch his scars, the spots where they removed tumors. He asks me about my health, "You should drink tea too, take a sip, my little sweetie." He pours some iced tea into my mouth then sticks his tongue in. I choke, which makes him laugh even louder. I straddle him. He always fucks me the same way, he pins his hands down on my lap, making me move up and down his big dick so fast I think I'll pass out each time. After two minutes, he grunts and takes the condom off, fully satisfied, and huddles up next to me.

Prudence, an escort working in another motel room, calls to offer me a slice of all-dressed pizza and she comes over to smoke a cigarette on my balcony. No one walks by on the street, the building is on a dead-end, it's so quiet. I laugh thinking that clients would find it surreal to see us sitting on white plastic chairs, me in my asymmetrical black skirt, red tank top, and thigh-high fishnet stockings and Prudence smoking a cigarette in a silver nightie with her new shiny tattoos on her well-exposed arms. She asks me if I know which agency Amber chose to work for and we talk about Vera, who stopped being an escort to become a buyer for Parasuco, a line of street clothes selling $600 jeans.

She borrows some clean linen before going back to her room. I'm expecting a client. I find him unpleasant from the start: he's fat, looks at me in a superior way, and has an annoying high-pitched voice. As soon as he tries to penetrate me, I tense up. "Are you stressed? Does it hurt?" I clench my fists and feel my plastic wedding ring against my palm, which relaxes me a bit. He leaves me his business card, he has an important job at Hewlett-Packard, and hopes I'll call him to see him outside of work. A guy who looks like a former colleague of mine at Archambault follows him in. I'm thinking of that colleague as he goes down on me and I climax, thinking of all the fights we had. I hated him, hated how he always hid books with erotic covers and talked about his faith as if God spoke to him every morning. Having his lookalike between my legs focusing on my clit and not Egon Schiele's drawings of prepubescent girls feels like a sweet revenge on my boring and sanctimonious former colleague.

I try to reach Samuel so he can take care of the faulty alarm system, and a new client wants me to jump on the bed with him. I find that a hoot but I'm scared of breaking the bed, wondering if this client has a fetish about pillow fights or if he's on ecstasy. Once lying down, our legs intertwined, he says I look open minded enough to do porn films. "I started a film production company about six months ago, I often go out to clubs with actresses and models, I'm going to spend the weekend at the Beach Club in Saint-Gabriel,[18] you should come too." I tell him I'm not a fan of the Beach Club. A friend's sister spent a day in a coma because a Beach Club guy put the drug GHB in her Sex on the Beach cocktail. And I'm not ready to be in a porn film yet, but pretending I'm Jenna Jameson just once might entertain me. So I write down his phone number and Website address and he leaves, after giving me a light spanking.

I have five more clients and I leave with a big envelope full of $20 bills in my gym bag. I meet up with Prudence at the bus stop, we sit next to each other on the crowded bus, and she starts talking about her clients, without lowering her voice. Though this first surprised me I find it refreshing and liberating to hear someone tell me about her client licking her armpits or her boyfriend releasing his first CD at the Diable Vert nightclub in a few days. I let my guard down without looking at anyone around us and confess, "Today, a client brought me a dildo, he wanted me to use it while he'd play with himself in front of me. It was a used dildo, not even in its box. He assured me he had washed it but yuck! I didn't let him use a sex-toy on me that already went in the pussy of another girl that I don't even know." Prudence giggles, "One of mine gave me the latest Harry Potter book, he's super nice, I love him, but he's weird, he talks about the CBC radio show host René Homier-Roy all the time, though he criticizes him for using the terms 'impressive' and 'breath taking' too much, he tries to impersonate him while fucking me."

I offer her a bubble-gum-flavored lollipop and she

---

18. Saint Gabriel is a village in the Lanaudière region of the province of Quebec, known for its beach. It's a ninety-minute drive from Montreal.

confides that she sometimes thinks she's not that popular at the agency, "I have too many tattoos and clients prefer nice little girls like you or Murielle. You know she's almost thirty?" Murielle looks like she's thirteen, her braided red hair and her spoiled-brat pout disturb me each time I see her. I let Prudence know what Debbie told me about Murielle, "She doesn't like being an escort, she says it's only nymphos who can do it without wanting to kill themselves, and she only does it because he father used to be a millionaire but lost all his money when she was almost eighteen. She doesn't want to change her lifestyle, she wants to keep horse-riding and buying $1,000 dresses. Her father's also pretending he's still rich, living in the same house, but it's empty, devoid of furniture, but it's worth millions. I'm sure selling it would help him out but he doesn't want to, he needs the neighbors to think he's still a successful business man." Prudence's eyes widen. "I'm not a nympho. And I don't need to see a shrink. I just like it and I better take advantage of it while I'm young, then one day I'll have lots of babies with my boyfriend. Maybe I'll go to university. Are you in school?" I tell her about my literature courses, confiding that I sometimes regret choosing that field, I should have chosen history, or communications, or anthropology. I don't feel as if I'm learning anything studying literature surrounded by students who think they're amazing because they spend their time in microbreweries and the only books they read are those the program deems mandatory.

Prudence stretches her legs and puts her feet up on the bus seat in front of her. "I used to accompany a friend to see clients. I didn't sleep with the guys, only going down on my friend. Then I decided to become an escort as well, but I find it more reassuring being in an agency than doing independent work." We kiss and promise to go out soon to laugh about girls who only climax once a year.

I wake up the next morning before the alarm clock rings,

my back and thighs aching, but feeling great. I notice the rain only when I step outside to get my July 5th copy of the newspaper *La Presse*. I'm surprised. I wanted to have breakfast with Samuel at Le Barbare. I suggest to Samuel that we wait a bit, but after thirty minutes it's still pouring, and the TV shows images of cars submerged in water. But it's hot and I want to go out. I take my umbrella, telling Samuel we should run to the restaurant. Outside, we're alone on the street. My pants get soaked all the way to my knees. I close my umbrella which barely offered shelter, my hair sticks to my face, I lose a shoe in a pond, and burst out laughing. I take Samuel's hand. "Save me, save me, I really want to have strawberry jam and toast." We finally get to Le Barbare. I roll up my pants and sit on my heels, barefoot.

Samuel orders a tall orange juice, some eggs, and bacon, while I ask for two orders of whole wheat toast. I take a few sips of his O.J. and suggest we invite Julien along with another one of his friends and Prudence to our apartment. I'm currently reading the Marguerite Duras biography written by Laure Adler and I'm fascinated. I want to be just like her and learn how to cook so friends will always hang around the apartment "We could even organize orgies. I have a super sexy client, Diamond, who used to own a swingers' club. And you could finally sleep with a girl who has big boobs."

# Bombs Exploding in London and in an Afterhours Club

I let my jeans lie around the living room floor, along with my lucky panties, the ones with a palm tree on them, and I turn on the TV before putting on a new black dress with a very low neckline I bought at Le Château. Reporters are talking at the same time, while the British flag is displayed in the corner of the screen. I stop what I'm doing and stand naked in front of the TV trying to understand what happened. Three bombs went off on the London Tube. I call Samuel, crying like everyone on TV, and inform him of the terrorist attacks, telling him I love him, completely astounded, knowing this will give me nightmares all week, just like after 9/11. I don't want to hang up or stop staring at the images on the screen, burnt bodies on stretchers succeeding one another. The reporters are forecasting at least fifty dead and five hundred wounded.

I try to regain control of myself, splashing some water on my face, and entertain Freddy, a fifty-something man who likes me very wet. He heard about the London attacks on the radio. He holds me in his arms, kissing my forehead, reassuring me with gentleman manners, and we watch TV. He smokes three cigarettes in a row and yells out in rage when the reporter informs the viewers about a fourth bomb exploding on a Tavistock Square bus. He wants me to give him a massage. As he lies on his tummy, I start with his left foot, counting to 120 then rubbing the right. I can hear Freddy snoring. I sit astride his back to massage his shoulders, which are full of mosquito bites. He wakes up with a hard-on, flips onto his back, wanting me to jerk him off. He inserts a finger into my pussy before putting it in his mouth. He asks me what my plans are for the coming weekend. I tell him I'm going to celebrate my parents' twentieth wedding anniversary. He says he doesn't believe in love. I'm offended "My parents really love each other, they're the cutest couple in the whole wide world, my mom's really independent, she works a lot but they bike and go to the theater every week together, my dad sometimes cooks for her, he makes spaghetti or chicken hamburgers. I swear they're beautiful to look at." He finds me naive. "I'm dating a twenty-five-year-old girl I met in a St. Laurent Street restaurant, and I know she's not with me because she loves me. She's with me because I have a big boat and money. I don't find her grateful enough, you make me come more often than she does." I wonder what his girlfriend thinks about escorts. I don't get girls who act like gold diggers but think being a whore is more degrading than lying about liking diamond bracelets.

David, my big-dicked client, comes to see me again, his knees full of bruises, and tells me he drank too much last night. "I danced on my knees in a Sherbrooke bar, my love." This time, he tears my pussy inch by inch, while I think about Londoners, reminding myself my pain is nothing. I insert some fingers in my pussy afterwards to check if I'm bleeding but I'm still intact. Tony Soprano gives me a pretty Kathy Van Zeeland handbag with the price tag still dangling from it. I subtly look and notice it's worth $130. He asks me if it shows that he's lost some weight. He looks nervous today with his abandoned puppy eyes. He says this may be our last meeting. He has to leave for New York City to take care of a problem and he doesn't know when he'll be back. I feel as if he's admitting that he has ties with the Mafia, which really makes me feel as if I'm in an episode of *The Sopranos*. He's super nice with me and says he wants to get to know me better before leaving, "You're the best in the world. I don't understand why you work here. Why? You're a beautiful girl-next-door type, you're normal, you don't do drugs. Aren't you scared sometimes of diseases? Do you do this so people will tell you you're pretty? Do you think you're good looking?" I'm surprised by his questions and giggle, asking him if he's currently reading a psychology book. He strokes my thigh. "No, I'm still reading the biography of the Red Hot Chili Peppers singer but I think about you a lot." I thank him for caring about me without really answering his questions. "I don't plan on being an escort long, I want to write children's books, but it's true that I like being told I'm pretty. Do you think I am?"

I make a face and pretend I have a squint. Tony Soprano shakes his head, trying to hide a smile. I wonder if it's possible to want too much to be loved. I don't know what my clients think of me after they leave the apartment, but I feel so good, close to them, useful, appreciated, and loved enough for them to call hours ahead to book an hour with me. Some offer me snacks of fresh produce while others give me designer handbags. I thank Tony Soprano, telling him to be careful in New York City. He leaves and I remain in the doorway watching him walk towards the elevator.

I watch the news on CNN while drinking green tea with only a teaspoon of honey. I hesitate, wondering if I should ask the next client, who doesn't look eighteen yet, for some ID. He fucks me while we're standing against a wall, his face devoid of any expression, then picks me up and brings me to the bed where he fucks me for a good thirty minutes before sighing, climaxing, and asking me, "Was I good? This was my first time." I feel nauseous. I don't like knowing I'm his first, I'm not like my friend Molly whose favorite fantasy is to be surrounded by virgin boys she could deflower them in a harem. I popped my first boyfriend's cherry in a bunk bed he shared with his twin brother and I deflowered Samuel, and I haven't kept any pleasant memories from these two experiences. I prefer older men who make me feel like I'm a beginner. I reassure my client and he tells me he watched lots of porn films to know what to do.

A premature ejaculator fucks me for thirty seconds, and I'm furious that he bit me so hard I'm going to have a purple bruise on the back of my neck. A guy with a dick piercing fucks me next and the condom bursts under the pressure of his Prince Albert, which really shocks me. Embarrassed, the client offers to give me more money but I tell him to forget it, and that he should warn the next girls to use two condoms. Richard, the former owner of a Repentigny pool room is my last client of the day. He gets me wet despite the ongoing London tragedy. He looks like a fitness-magazine model with his chiseled face, his muscular arms, and a hard dick coming and going inside my pussy as if it were put on this Earth just to fuck me. He makes me scream. The bed-on-wheels rolls, which makes us laugh, and he licks my ear while we do it doggy-style. I try to catch my breath but he doesn't slow down, fucking me non-stop for a good half hour.

I leave without taking a shower, with lubricant and pussy juice stuck to my thighs and the smell of Richard's perfume, Swiss Army, on my body. I wrap the presents I plan on giving my parents on behalf of my brothers and me for their wedding anniversary. I fill a suitcase with ten bikinis, white dresses to show off my tan and yellow patent leather platform sandals. I also pack Samuel's suitcase and call my dad to find out what time he'll come get me tomorrow so we'll head out together to our family cabin in a lovely village in the Laurentians.

Once at the cabin, I kiss my brothers, who find me very cute in my canary-yellow shorts from Pink, and I tell them to shave their chin hairs while stealing my brother Philippe's Dolce & Gabbana shades. Samuel is off to ride on a Sea-Doo while I pick raspberries with my mom and sunbathe while sucking on a Mr. Freeze. I tell everyone that tomorrow we'll have to get up early because I made reservations for brunch at the Auberge Mont-Gabriel. My parents tell me I shouldn't have, but I hug them and tell them they deserve as many crêpes filled with fruit and whipped cream as they can eat. My father makes me listen to some Joe Dassin and my Philippe confides in me that he cheated on his girlfriend with a girl he met at a bar when he was totally drunk and has been guilt ridden ever since. I tell him I'll pray his girlfriend will forgive him and he asks me when exactly I started believing in God. I can't tell him it's because I fuck two dozen men each week, and that they're all nice to me, never hitting me or robbing me. I explain that I started reading the new ecumenical translation of the Bible and feel inspired, close to God and Jesus' kindness.

At night, we make a campfire and I burn my marshmallows. Samuel huddles up next to me but I push him away. I want to be alone, even with my family present, I want to feel as if the fire's burning just for me, that the forest surrounding me and the couple of loons on the water are mine only. While we're having brunch the next day, I go to the bathroom every five minutes to check that my belly's not bloated from eating too much bacon. Not much of a coffee-drinker, I get a headache from having too many cups of Joe. I pay the maître d' the $100 bill, congratulating my parents a thousand times for their lasting union. I know I won't stay married to Samuel as long as them. I can't stand his family or his long hair that he refuses to cut although I keep encouraging him by showing him pictures of Colin Farrell and Johnny Depp, I need a man who wants me all to himself. I'm exhausted. I find all the men who pay me more admirable than him.

When I return from my family weekend, I do two hours of aerobics while watching *Six Feet Under* episodes, after which I go shopping in a sex shop. I need Japanese condoms, a Rabbit vibrator, and another schoolgirl uniform. While I am browsing in the porn film aisle, the saleswoman tells me all about her favorite porn stars and about porn film dubbing, "I'd love to get paid to go ooh, ahh, and 'Go in deeper!' all day." I buy a Marc Dorcel film and listen to the woman behind the cash register talk to another saleswoman about her new Pug dog she called James Dean. I call Samuel and ask him to meet me at the travel agency, where we pay for our California plane tickets in cash. We'll stay five days at the Georgian Hotel, an Art deco establishment in Santa Monica, and two nights at the Holiday Inn located thirty seconds from Venice Beach.

In the afternoon, we attend a showing of the movie *Mr. & Mrs. Smith*. I find all these guns exciting and tell Samuel I must learn to fire a gun in a shooting range. I bump into Prudence outside the Quartier Latin theater, and she invites me to join her and some of her girlfriends at a tapas restaurant before going out dancing at Stereo, an afterhours club in the Gay Village. We decide to meet at Stereo at midnight. I'm excited at the thought of having girlfriends. I miss Misha, Molly, Laurie, my cousin, all of whom I haven't seen in ages, too busy applying self-tanning lotion and being businessmen's dirty little lunch hour secret to think about them.

I'm wearing a dress I bought at the Frivole store,

it's super cute full of unicorns and multicolored hearts. Prudence finds me irresistible, "I should force you to get undressed and give me your dress!" She introduces me to her two girlfriends and we go into Stereo holding hands. She kisses the doorman. The room is full of smoke and men in white T-shirts. It's dark. I decide to have fun and pretend I'm used to these types of places and living Paris Hilton's life every night. I'm dancing, my throat is really dry, and a guy tries to talk to me, but I can't hear anything he's saying because of the loud music. He takes me by the waist, pulls me towards him, and kisses me. I close my eyes, a bit dizzy, and tell him I'm thirsty. He orders a bottle of Grey Goose vodka and shares it with me. Prudence teases me, "He's ugly as shit and he's kissed half the girls here before you. Come, I'll introduce you to another girlfriend. I'm sure you two will get along."

Karen's gorgeous. She looks a bit like Kate Hudson with her vintage almost see-through bohemian dress. We dance and share a gin and tonic into which she plunges her finger before inserting it into my mouth. We sit on a leather seat and start kissing. She takes my breasts out of my dress and a security guard warns us to stop it. We laugh and pretend we're shamed but Karen's too drunk, she jumps on me and we fall from the seat onto the dance floor. My arm hurts. I stay sprawled on the floor, my dress raised up to my bellybutton, and we get kicked out of the club. I didn't even get a chance to tell Prudence. Karen takes me by the arm and kisses me on the mouth in front of all the party animals on St. Catherine Street. She suggests we go back to her place. I ask her if it's close by but can't hear her reply. I decide to follow her anyway. She pins me against store windows and shows me what she'd like to buy, giving me painful hickies on my neck. I tell her to stop but she continues anyway.

We've been walking for ten minutes when she takes an

alcohol flask out of her purse and downs it, pretending not to remember where she lives. I'm starting to get tired and I tell her I'm going to hop into a taxi and go sleep at home, but she swears we're close to her apartment. When we get there, her roommates are playing poker by candlelight. She doesn't introduce me. I'm wondering if she even remembers my name. She puts some music on in her bedroom, and while I sit on her bed and look at her, she comes between my legs. "You smell good." She takes off my panties, biting the inside of my thighs. I'm starting to worry she's going to bite my clitoris, but she becomes gentler and goes down on me with little flicks of her tongue. I ask her to sit on me on her bed but she doesn't want to. She shows me her panties where I make out a maxi pad. At that very moment I want a dick. I wonder if I could ask her to invite one of her roommates to join us but decide against it. I think about my English client, picturing him next to us, threatening to slap me if I don't climax. He touches me, shows me how hard he can get by watching me with another girl, and warns me he's about to ejaculate on my face and my mouth so I can taste him, but also my eyes, so it'll sting. He wants me to be in pain, to feel it burn my eyes, and he calls me a little bitch. I arch my back and scream, Karen's fist in my mouth.

She offers me something to drink and I follow her to the kitchen where I see all the dirty glasses by the sink and politely decline. She says she really wants to become my best friend because I have the softest pussy in the whole world, but I write down a wrong number in her one-year-old McGill student agenda.

# The Shame of Knowing More About Jennifer Aniston than About Gaudí

I buy some gray suits and high-waisted skirts for when I go back to school. I want to look more serious yet sluttier than all my female professors. I also buy some folder with Barbie on them. The first week of classes is my favorite. The professors rarely give three-hour-long lectures, the vending machines' hot chocolate seems delicious, and I like guessing which student gained weight during the summer and which ones wear push-up bras. I am taking a beginner Spanish class this semester and the girl sitting next to me in class, to whom I have to say *te llamas* ten times, is a gorgeous Asian girl. She likes gossip magazines and aerobics as much as I do, and I blush just thinking about going to the gym with her, watching her undress in the locker room.

On Sunday, just to forget the fact that summer's coming to an end and I'll soon have to stop applying self-tanning lotion on a daily basis, I go with Samuel and Julien to the Tam-Tams on Mount Royal. Each Sunday, from the time the last snows have melted in the spring until October or even November, hundreds of people mostly dressed in a hippie fashion bring their tam-tams, their ten grams of weed, their dogs, kids, or circus equipment and they dance, play music, juggle, or look at the asses of hippies doing body painting.

We walk on Mont-Royal Street on our way to the mountain, and I stop at the Goth store Cruella to look at some lingerie and long satin gloves and vow to come back later to try on their leather minis. I really don't feel as if I belong when Julien starts sharing his pineapple with lots of strangers while I'm lying on a beach towel, my denim shorts showing off the G-string sticking out of my crack. I watch Samuel rolling a joint and girls wearing dreadlocks. With my *Vanity Fair* and my *Marie Claire*, I don't fit in. I feel out of place everywhere except in a bed. This doesn't sadden me, it just makes me feel as if I should flip through my Paperblanks notebook and call a client like that Swiss guy who owns a condo in Old Montreal. I could ask him to give me $1,000 to spend the weekend with him, try some of his coke, and worry I'd become a different person if I like it. I'd blow him for six hours if I needed to, hoping he'd talk to me non-stop about the other girls he fucked, or his inheritance, or his favorite restaurants.

With my purse worth more than a tam-tam, more than twenty grams of weed, I decide to go for a walk and follow guys walking their dogs and I bump into Geneviève, the girlfriend I had seen at the Berri-UQAM metro station a month ago. She introduces me to her friends, super cute guys who should cut their long hair, just like Samuel, and she asks me if I know anyone selling poppers. I tell her I don't and leave to buy a strawberry-kiwi Popsicle. When I find Samuel, he looks as if he's in a trance, playing on his tam-tam. He invites me to dance like the dozen people in front of him, but I stick my nose up in the air like one of those stuck-up bitches in the movie *Mean Girls* and tell him I'm going shopping instead, and that I'll meet him at the apartment with some prepared meals from Ripaille et Bombance. I notice Samuel's not wearing one of the new T-shirts I bought him and I'm disappointed. I don't like his old Smashing Pumpkins T-shirt he's had forever. It's dirty, faded, and full of holes.

I go back to Cruella where I buy a red wig, with which I want to surprise Samuel tonight, and a royal blue latex dress. The salesman, in platform shoes, goes into raptures over my waistline, "You should wear corsets, you could lose two more inches and be exceptional!" When Samuel and Julien arrive home, I tell them what the salesperson said, very proud of myself, pretending to be Dita Von Teese's twin sister, but they don't react. Samuel tells me I look pretty as a redhead while Julien says I look like a drag queen.

I don't feel like going to work. I ate some bacon-flavored chips for the first time in a year with Samuel and his friend yesterday. I feel ugly. I'm bloated. I have my period and a zit on my chin. I bought myself the second season of the TV show *The O.C.* just before my dad came by this afternoon to fix my kitchen shelves. He's so nice to me, he lives an hour away and comes by just to do me a favor and notice I still can't make coffee. I wish Samuel was more like my father sometimes, that he'd own a toolbox and know how to use all the different kinds of screwdrivers instead of playing guitar and knowing all The Doors' songs by heart.

I get to the apartment a little before 5 P.M. Hélène's happy to leave early, she's been busy all day and needs to rest because she has to work in Dorval tomorrow. She's beaming and looks way better than she did last time I saw her. She tells me she just started working again after spending the last two months as a waitress helping her mother in her Eastern Townships restaurant. I insert a contraceptive sponge as far up my pussy as I can and proceed to wash myself, making sure there's no more blood on my lips or thighs. I break the medicine cabinet's mirror while putting away my makeup and start swearing. I wonder if I should tell Debbie or pretend that another escort had broken it prior to my arrival. Alain's my first client. He tells me he slept only three hours last night. I tell him he has fewer rings around his eyes than I do. "Do you hide them with concealer?" I brush my finger around his eyes and kiss him on tip toe. He undresses me while kissing the back of my neck, my breasts, my ass cheeks. I'm annoyed by his fleshy lips. I'd like to have them around my clit but I can't ask him that. He lies down on the bed and asks me to come on top of him. I lick his balls and he looks at me, "I'd like you to kiss me on the mouth," asking me as if it were something intimate, not suspecting I don't mind and kiss almost all my clients. I lean over him and become nervous, knowing he sees this first kiss as important. I kiss him. He inserts both his tongue and dick in me while we kiss and I moan, my lips wide open, loving his violent and unpredictable tongue.

He pushes me aside so he can come over me, as he pulls out of my pussy I notice at the same time as he does the blood on the condom. I'm ashamed and start apologizing, not able to look him in the face, but he plunges back between my legs. "Stop, it's natural, your cunt's soft, let me take advantage of it, calm down. How does my cock feel? Do you want it back inside you?" I bite my lips, "Fuck me." He pinches each of my nipples, pulling on them with his teeth before collapsing next to me on the bed. Leaning on my elbows, I look at the blond and gray hairs on his chest, see his face red from exhaustion. He asks me about my studies and notices how anguished I am over them. "Why don't you drop out? I enjoy my freedom too much to do things I don't like. Couldn't you just write, what do you think a bachelor degree will bring you? I can't imagine you teaching, my angel." This brings tears to my eyes. If only he knew how much I want to drop out, but I want that diploma to reward the efforts I put in showing up to half my classes.

We talk about traveling. He likes border towns such as

Foz do Iguaçu at the westernmost point of Brazil, Argentina, and Paraguay, and Tijuana in Mexico, where you can hear shots being fired, drink tequila, gamble, and listen to the music of macabre celebrations. "I played a Mexico game, a dice game of chance and strategy, the main purpose of it is to meet incredible people who call you a *hijo de puta* or *cabrón* when they lose, but embrace you *con su hermano* when the game's over." He also talks about his two-year-old girl. His eyes sparkle when he talks about her. He says she was staying over at his place last night, he's just bought a condo in the St. Henri neighborhood by the Atwater Market and the Lachine Canal bike path but it's not yet furnished. "We slept on an inflatable mattress and she kicked me all night." As soon as he leaves, I find myself stupid for only listening to him without telling him what I think of border towns or Proudhon's philosophy because I honestly don't know what it is. I'm sure he won't be back because I know more about Jennifer Aniston than about Gaudí.

Mark, a West Island Anglophone in his thirties, follows Alain. After asking me to blow him down on my knees, he tells me he's a newlywed who hasn't sought the company of escorts for the last six months. "I'm glad I chose you. You're the best." He gives me a $30 tip.

Debbie calls, warning me Vera was just battered by a client, "He stole all her money. He asked her to give him all of it, she refused, and they got into a fight. Brandon thinks the hallway camera got him and he'll go after him. These types of guys don't just hit one agency. I'll call the others so they can warn their girls. He's white as a sheet, has a shaved head, wears a hoodie, and has a dirty old gray backpack with him." I ask if Vera's hurt. Debbie says she will probably have a black eye and went back home to rest. Eve should come fill in for her within the hour so I won't be left alone to satisfy all the clients in need of a hairless pussy. I always hide my money in three different places at the agency, under the mattress, in my makeup bag, and in a take-out menu for a downtown restaurant. I would never argue with a robber, I'd give him all my bills, but only from one of my hiding places.

A gorgeous guy in his early forties wearing a light pink polo shirt knocks at the door. He says he chose me because he loves black-haired girls with small breasts. He fucks me on all fours, holding on to my thighs, "Can you raise your ass a little bit please?" He gets dressed as soon as he's climaxed. He thanks me, saying how much he appreciates the agency's services, because despite not having time to be in a relationship he often needs to empty his sack. After he's gone, I check to see if my new sponge is still inserted well up my cunt and if I'm clean. I was so relieved by Alain's reaction earlier, but I fear not all my clients would be as calm as he was with an escort on her period. I open my arms to greet John, the New York State prison warden. He gives me burned copies of the latest Stéphanie Lapointe and Camille CDs and I thank him. He feels so fragile in my arms, I wonder how he can dominate the prisoners in his care and the guards who work for him. He comes over me, tickling my face with his salt-and-pepper mustache, and rests his head between my legs, near my cunt, telling me he bought two tickets for the Mylène Farmer concert in Paris that's scheduled for late December. "I don't have anyone to go with. Would you like to accompany me?" I tell him I'll think about it, but "December is still far away. I'm sure you'll find someone else to invite by then, John. But if you don't, maybe, a weekend in Paris... you'd force me to eat lots of croissants and wear a beret? I'd have to practice speaking with a French accent first!"

I hear my cell phone go off while I'm in the shower, and I answer quickly, spilling water all over the floating wooden floor. Debbie tells me a new client's on his way. I dry myself and straighten my hair with an iron. As soon as I let him in, the client says he'd like me to dominate him. "If you don't feel up to it or if you don't want to, let me know, it's okay." I confess I've never tried being a dominatrix but I'm ready to give it a shot if he can give me directions. Being dominant is so unnatural to me I wonder if I won't get the giggles asking him to lick my heels. He undresses and lies down on the floor. "Do you have another pair of shoes?" I show him my naughty secretary stilettos. He asks me to wear them and to walk all over his body. I narrow my eyes so I won't look too much like a wide-eyed naive doe and step on his tummy. He doesn't say a word, as if he didn't feel pain. He tells me to sit on him, my back on his face and put as much weight as I can on him while kicking him in the balls with my heels. I call him a bastard and a jerk and he likes it, telling me to go on. I kick him harder, "Shut up!" I don't feel like my usual self, wondering what I should say and do next, but being an overpowering slut amuses me. He's very calm, encouraging me to sit on his face, "If you please, mistress. I know I don't deserve it." I stand up, driving my heels into his ribcage and I sit over his face, telling him to stick his tongue out, beg me, and tell me my pussy smells wonderful. I tell him to lower his eyes and never look at me while speaking to me.

I give him my cunt to lick and I don't make a peep that could indicate I like it. After a few minutes I complain, "Your tongue's awful. Are you kidding me? How dare you not try to please me? You're useless. You should be ashamed of yourself. I never want you to go down on me again." He asks for my forgiveness, "I'm sorry, I didn't mean any disrespect Please give me another chance." Having no imagination whatsoever, I don't know what punishment to give him. I take off my stilettos and tell him to suck my heels like it's a guy's cock. Just before doing so, my slaves smiles at me and says, "Would it excite you if I sucked a guy's cock before you, mistress? I've done it before. I don't hate it, especially if I do so obeying a woman's orders." I push my heel into his mouth, choking him, and I realize this is giving him a hard-on. I take his cock in my hands, pinching it, slapping it, making it my toy, but since I can't laugh at it, it soon bores me.

I tell the guy to stand up. I put both my hands on the mattress, spread my legs, and raise my ass. "Make me come now. If you don't succeed, I'll leave you like this and you'll have to hide your ridiculous hard cock in your underwear." He promises to do a great job going down on me so maybe he'll get the chance to penetrate me later. I'm sure a real dominatrix doesn't let her client penetrate her and would humiliate him further before granting him an orgasm. He sucks my clitoris and I pretend I'm climaxing to make him happy. I climb on top of him. "Don't move, let me feel your dick deep inside my cunt, and ask for my permission before squirting cum in me." I shove a finger into his mouth so he'll suck it as if he were a baby and I tell him to orgasm already because being on top of him bores me. "Your dick's too small, I can't feel it." Afterwards he kisses me. "I sometimes go to swingers' clubs. I'm sure you'd like it." He gives me his business card, he's a realtor, and I tell him I might go with him one day if he promises there'll be more than one girl for thirty guys in this club.

I leave the agency with Eve. She calls her cats and leaves them a message on the voice mail. She shows me pictures of the five cats. She says she's mad at me because I kiss clients. "You're not supposed to do it for free. Then clients think all the escorts do it. I ask $20 extra for that." I think she's being ridiculous, kissing clients makes this job feel less mechanical, more real and exciting, but I respect Eve, a blondie I suspect of being underage, when she's actually twenty-seven and has been an escort for the last five years.

At the apartment, Samuel tells me my mother phoned.

I call her back the next day and she says we should have dinner together. We have lamb and blue cheese hamburgers at Folies. We talk about my grandfather who sometimes thinks my father's his brother and got lost the other day and drove all the way to Trois-Rivières, which is a three-hour drive from his house. My grandmother didn't want to call the police, fearing they'd suspend his driver's license. My mother finishes my fries, dipping them in ketchup, before asking me if I'll be there on Thursday night when one of my brothers is leaving for Katimavik in Ontario, a youth volunteer-service program for seventeen to twenty-one-year-old Canadians. I tell her I'll miss Philippe and will buy him a wide-eyed plush pig.

# Round Doll Eyes Like Olives
## in Tanqueray Gin

Last time I was with Alain, we had talked about the controversial caricatures of Muhammad in a Danish newspaper. We had fucked three times, which resulted in my pussy being sore all day, and he had left me his phone number. I had written it down on a page of the free newspaper *24 H*, and now in between classes I'm sitting on some steps in the design pavilion of the university with that torn newspaper page in my hands. I'm nervous when I call him. He answers, warning me he's in an elevator, and says he'll come get me tonight, we'll have dinner at Doval, a Portuguese restaurant he loves.

I skip my last class and head back home, tell Samuel I'm going out tonight, and try on a thousand different outfits in front of him. I finally opt for a gold and white brocade miniskirt, a white shirt, and a nice little girl's cardigan. When Alain rings the doorbell, I quickly head downstairs, warning Samuel not to look at us through the window as I spit out my mint-flavored gum into my Kathy Van Zeeland purse. Alain says a friend of his lent him his Mercedes. I tell him I don't care about cars and don't know anything about them. He laughs and says, "Same here. I've never been the type to read *The Car Guide*." At the restaurant, he orders grilled sardines and mussels which we share. I'm hungry but don't touch the bread. He doesn't either. I don't want to look impolite or too greedy. We drink some white wine, toasting the success of escort agencies.

I ask him how he heard of Dream&Cream. He tells me he went to check online sites after splitting up with his wife. "Marlene gave me the idea. We broke up on my birthday. Now I can say it was a very nice gift, but she thought the breakup would help us get perspective, that it would prove her right. She always thought she knew better, that she was a relationship expert because she watched all the Oprah Winfrey and Dr. Phil shows. I was sexually frustrated, it didn't take me long to find someone else. I like solitude but don't like to be alone. Well-meaning friends, though lacking some judgment, told Marlene I was seeing another woman. She made a terrible scene, accusing me of seeing whores. Her insults made me think of seeking professional services to avoid any future conflict until the storm had passed." I decide against telling him about Samuel. Alain takes my hand, "My little brat, I have such deep affection for whores. I don't want to seem vulgar when I say this. My father was a dentist and when he started his business in France he set up by Réaumur-Sébastopol. You heard of Pigalle? It's only for the tourists. Réaumur-Sébastopol is where real prostitution is in Paris. I think he set up there to take advantage of low rent and a clientele who always paid him cash. My parents divorced when I was eight and when we visited him, my brothers and I, we went to his office. I'd wait with the whores in the waiting room while my brothers played outside. I preferred staying with the ladies of the evening who were beautiful or not, young or not, but always kind to me, making a fuss over me, and I'd sit on everybody's lap."

He doesn't stop pouring me white wine and I listen to him without talking, so it's not until we've left the restaurant and I've lost a shoe on the street that I notice I'm plastered.

He drives us to Le Manoir. "The barmaids are gorgeous and they're all studying at the HEC,[19] hoping to meet a rich man." But the club's closed on Mondays. He suggests we go to my place to fuck but I refuse, using its messiness as an excuse. He says he doesn't mind, having once lived in a squat with punk friends. I tell him I can blow him in the Mercedes. I sit on him and kiss him while he strokes my hair and unbuttons my blouse. He pulls on my nipples and I have to keep from screaming. I can feel him becoming hard against my brocade skirt, and I raise it and fumble to unzip his pants but can't manage to. He says he can't bring me to his apartment either. He only has that mattress and it might deflate with each pelvis thrust. He calls the friend who used to put him up during the breakup with Marlene and we drive to Habitat 67. I'm impressed at the thought of going to that housing complex designed by architect Moshe Safdie and used by many foreign dignitaries as a temporary residence during the Expo 67. I shyly say hello to Alain's friend who's sitting at the dinner table with his wife and some friends, while Alain and I walk towards the bedroom. As I undress, Alain asks me to keep my La Senza boyish peach-colored panties on and he fucks me while looking at us in the mirror. We doze off, then we fuck some more before he goes down on me. Short of breath, he tells me it's not fair, girls only need a cute little ass like mine to be irresistible when guys have to charm girls by acting like perfect gentlemen and being able to talk about art, architecture, love, literature, and how to grow tomatoes. I giggle and make him suck on one of my fingers while stroking his belly with my long hair before putting his dick in my mouth. He drives me home at 6 A.M. Samuel's waiting for me, worried. I apologize for getting home so late and fall asleep smelling of Clinique Happy fragrance and most probably latex and pussy juice.

The next morning, I vomit just before going to the Jean-

19. Hautes Études Commerciales, top Montreal business school

Talon Market with my mother. Alain leaves a message on my voice mail saying he really liked our evening together. I'm delighted to hear this and I listen to the message five times before calling him back. I tell him I just bought big cucumbers with my mother and old fashioned donuts, and that my kitten Minuit[20] is sucking his daddy Syphilis' teats right before me. Alain tells me about an exhibition of painter Claude Gauvreau's work, and asks me to come see it with him on Wednesday night, "You can even come by my place first, I now have an armchair, an IKEA table and some chairs, I'll make us dinner." Not having to work till Thursday, I'm happy to accept his invitation. I'm not sure what I feel for Alain but I find him too interesting to see him only at the agency. I don't want to tell Samuel, because I know it'll hurt him to know I enjoy spending even my leisure time with clients, so instead I tell him I'll go sleep at my cousin's, too feverish at the thought of spreading my legs for Alain's big cock to feel any guilt.

Alain picks me up by the university, telling me how boring his business lunch was, all he could think about were my panties. I sigh, "I feel lost in my Literature and Society class, I don't care for Balzac and don't understand Auerbach, Marx, or the Cénacle.[21] I cross my fingers. If I do it hard enough it'll work, I'll pass the exam, I swear." We stop at the Première Moisson bakery at the Atwater Market to buy some raspberry pastries. Once at his place, he lights a fire in the fireplace. It's already getting cold outside and I'll soon need to buy a new faux-fur-trimmed corduroy coat and an angora wool scarf at Simons. His empty condo seems huge. He tells me to sit in his Victorian armchair and spread my legs, raises my denim skirt, and licks my twat while staring at me, proud to see me squirm. Not knowing what to do

20. Literally *Midnight*
21. Parisian literary group around the time of the French Revolution

with my arms and legs, I put my hands underneath my ass and push his head away. "I think we'll go see the Gauvreau exhibit some other time." He nods, "I had no plans to go... the exhibit's on for a month so we have plenty of time." He lowers his pants and I watch him jerk off, his tongue against my clit.

He changes his clothes, keeping his light blue and white striped shirt but slipping on a pair of jeans. He puts on some punk music followed by some Manu Chao and translates one of Castro's speeches for me, singing while cooking. He puts the armchair in front of the counter so I can face him, goes and gets a paperback copy of *One Hundred Years of Solitude*. "I read it while I was vacationing in South America. I used it as a pillow on many occasions, that's why it's worn out and the cover page is missing." We have some meunière-style sole with polenta which fills me up but he insists on feeding me spoonfuls of the raspberry pastries. He then draws me a bath and I enter it with a dry martini while he does the dishes. I drink it slowly, not wanting to get drunk, and I find the olives have an exquisite taste soaked in Tanqueray gin. I sink my head underwater and I no longer hear Alain's music. I feel great. I'd stay like this a long time if only I wouldn't drown.

Alain joins me. I spill some of my martini while we toast. He finds the water too hot. I kiss him. He tells me while adding cold water to the tub, "Sometimes I wish you would be mine, not mine but with me and nobody else. But I know I'm too old and mostly too stupid. I have too many women in my life. I wish I could have only one. Maybe if I were ten years younger. But nothing in the world could make me want to relive these last ten years." I start blowing him and he stops me. "What do you want to do later, what will you like doing after you're no longer an escort?" I start to cry. I've already had too much to drink, and I hate thinking about my studies or my future. "I don't know. Sorry. I used to want to become a teacher or write children's books, or become a hypnotherapist, but now I have no clue." He takes me into his arms. "You can be whatever you want to be." And I cry, knowing very well I can't. I can't be a respectable girl, I can't say how old I really am, I can't love, I can no longer feel love, I can't get straight A's anymore in school, I can't be the perfect girl my parents would want me to be, I can't be as pretty as Kimber in *NipTuck*. We stay a long while in the bath tub. Alain gets up from time to time to make himself another martini, putting a dozen olives in his glass. I stroke his dick with my feet, which makes him hard. He sits on the side of the bath tub and I blow him. He tells me this won't do, he wants my pussy. I step out of the tub, shivering. He puts his bathrobe around my shoulders. I look at my face reddened by tears in the mirror. I'm not scary looking, I just seem incredibly fragile, like the tips of my hair. I'll never be pretty, but I feel like I am, on the inflatable mattress, giggling from the noise it makes when I bounce on it.

He climbs on top of me. "Are you clean?" I look at him, unsure of what he's saying. "Are you sure you don't have any disease? I'd like to feel you around me, without a latex barrier." I tell him I agree, and that I'm clean, that each month a Stella nurse tells me I'm in perfect health, my blue veins are super easy to puncture, and my pussy's clean without a trace of crabs or herpes. I hold my breath when he plunges inside me. "You have the eyes of a doll who doesn't seem to know if what she's going through is real." I feel like crying again. Nobody, not even Samuel, makes love to me like this anymore. We always practice safe sex and I didn't remember my pussy could get this wet opening and closing as much. We fall asleep. I sleep poorly on his inflatable mattress, tucked under a wool blanket raised all the way up to my forehead, his arms around me.

He drives me home very early the next morning before going to work. We kiss at each traffic light. Samuel's not home, having already left for class. Minuit meows, wanting to be petted, but as soon as I oblige, he runs away to go scratch on the red velvet couch. I nap for an hour before scheduling an appointment at Spa Diva for a facial massage and another one with hot stones, ordering two oak bookcases on IKEA's Website, and writing Alain to tell him, "Thanks for letting your sperm squirt between my thighs, I had forgotten how it felt to be wet down to my mid-thighs afterwards. Thanks for taking a bath with me, I wish I could have stayed in it for hours, and for showing me mathematics and logic books, for talking to me about Casanova and the Cyrillic alphabet, and thanks for showing me that if you put an onion under cold running water before slicing it, you won't cry. Thanks for staying up so late listening to me and telling me you like sleeping next to me."

I shave, my foot against the bathroom counter. Porcelaine stares at me. I dip a toasted pita into a jar of baba ganoush, while I check to see if I have new emails or comments on the MERB Website, I listen to some Goldfrapp before taking a cab to the agency. Apartment 408 is vacant so I set up, get dressed without turning on the TV. I'm wearing a black and pink sequined dress and knee-high socks under my fuck-me boots. I read a few pages of Chuck Klosterman's *Sex, Drugs and Cocoa Puffs: A Low Culture Manifesto*, and a new client arrives. He has broad shoulders, brown hair, and a sad smile when he tells me he's married with kids but no longer finds his wife attractive.

He stays two hours with me, going down on me until I come, then I climb on top of him and we kiss. He gently strokes my legs and belly and holds onto my ass. He's so nice, tuned into my every desire and every move, that I'm shocked to find out he got arrested last week for road rage. He stepped out of his car and punched the driver who had cut him off. The police intervened and he now has to attend anger management classes. "I had a bad day. I'm a professor at Concordia. I know it's not an excuse, I know I shouldn't have done it, I don't know what came over me." He wants to go down on me again. I warn him I'm not sure I can climax a second time and go to the bathroom. When I come back, he's giggling. "I heard you pee. It's stupid but I find it funny." I tease him, calling him an overgrown kid while pushing his head towards my pussy. When he leaves, he says he'd like to spend a whole day with me. A Polish man fucks me next. He has freckles all over his body and large, heavy hands. He tells me a thousand times that Canada's the best country in the world. I can picture him with an arrow sash and a Canada tattoo on his ass, and that turns me off completely.

Daniel, another client, goes down on me, but I don't like his fingers. He inserts one then two of them into my pussy. He drives them into me, which makes me back up against the bed. He comes over me saying he likes my black socks. "You're dressed like a nice little whore." As he puts his clothes back on, he talks to me about his three kids and the book *The Pillars of the Earth*. I find him insufferable. I absentmindedly listen to him, as rigid as a statue. I don't want Debbie to call to tell me I stay with my clients too long, but I don't know how to hurry him out. I then welcome Bruce, holding a nail file in my hands that I inattentively throw onto the kitchen counter. He calls me "his mistress" and wants to eat me out, but I'm starting to feel that my clit's too sensitive so I refuse and lie down on my tummy. He comes inside me while pulling on my hair. He wishes me a good night saying, "This must be a tough job. Good luck!" I close the door and yawn, wondering if I should call Samuel.

Around 9:30 P.M., I recognize Alain's voice on the

intercom. I smile right away and run to look at my reflection in the mirror, scenting myself with Very Irresistible perfume. He doesn't take his long black coat off right away, ardently kissing me instead with his eyes closed while mine remain open. He says he missed me already. "I just finished painting a room, it's not the right color, I'll have to repaint it later, and I found some black hair everywhere, on the walls, in the paint, on my fingers. I loved it. Each time I found one, I smiled and thought of you. I can't wait for you to come take a bath at my place again." I feel the same way he does. I would have preferred going back to his apartment, instead of his coming here to the agency, and talking for hours in his bath tub. He fucks me and when he takes the condom off, he drops it and all his cum drips out, hitting the floor with a strange noise. I giggle. The room will smell like cum till midnight. He wipes his mess with some tissues. He apologizes and leaves about ten minutes later, exhausted. His daughter will be visiting him tomorrow and he doesn't want to look like a zombie to her.

The client who had invited me to join him in the Bahamas pays me a call. He inserts a finger into my ass and climaxes as soon as he starts wiggling it around in there. He stays with me in the kitchen, smoking a cigarette while I drink some Matcha green tea. He asks me what classes I'm taking this semester and guesses how bored I am with the university. He tells me he used to skip a lot of classes and came up with lots of excuses for not showing up to exams or handing in his papers late. "I'd go to a funeral home, stay there a while, and grab a bookmark with the name of the deceased written on it, and I'd ask the funeral director to write me a note attesting that I was indeed present at the wake of a loved one." I thank him for sharing this excuse with me but I would never dare lie to one of my professors, too scared of a karmic retribution. Alone again, I almost feel like sleeping at the agency, in clean sheets. I don't want to go back to Samuel, play Scrabble while eating two-day-old red tuna sushi until he'd go smoke a last cigarette on the sly in the alley before joining me in bed, our bodies three feet apart.

# Relying Only on my Brat Smile and the Next Victoria's Secret Catalog

It's cold when I get up. The heating doesn't work properly and the windows aren't well insulated. I take a hot shower and hear my neighbors listening to the news on the radio. I go get the *La Presse* newspaper barefoot, without my slippers or my ballerina shoes, my naked body barely hidden behind a pink bath towel. I pour some almond and dried strawberry cereal into a bowl and find Minuit meowing at the back of the entrance closet. I'm not sure if I'll go to my contemporary dance class this afternoon or if I'll go shopping instead for new winter boots, nighties, and warm waterproof clothing so I can continue running outside even when the temperature drops below 15°F.

I huddle up in an armchair under a zebra-print throw in front of the huge window overlooking St. Denis Street and read Evelyn Lau's *Other Women*. I'm touched by this book way more than by Zola's or Balzac's, which I must read for my classes. It's about a woman who's a married man's mistress. He makes her miserable and doesn't care about her, even though she threatens him or eats so much she pukes. He doesn't want to make love to her, he only wants her lips on his cock, so she blows him. Though she had never felt any pleasure from it in the past, blowing him makes her happy. He opens her shirt and touches her breasts but when she wants to sit on him and feel his cock inside her, he refuses, telling her he'd already warned her this would never happen, they're only friends not lovers.

Alain invites me to drop by his place tonight and I'm delighted to accept. I down two Guru Lite energy drinks to make sure I'll be in top shape, and do 200 sit-ups and some weight training following the advice given by the private trainer of many Hollywood stars, Gunnar Peterson, in the November issue of *Glamour*. I read the new comments my clients have left on the MERB Website and I'm very proud of myself, they're all good. "I saw Marissa last week on my lunch hour and you were all right, Marissa's unique!! It was my fourth time at the Dream&Cream agency and by far my best experience. She flashed me such an amazing smile when I arrived. We undressed. She started by giving me a GREAT blow job (and licking my balls) and we fucked in different positions. I asked her if she could make me climax with her magic mouth. We talked a bit afterwards and she was adorable! I can't wait to see her again next week."

I'm wearing hot pink pantyhose and a white geisha dress when I ring Alain's doorbell, happy I didn't get lost trying to find his place in the dark. He opens the door in a bathrobe, and apologizes, saying he didn't have time to change. I kiss him "Don't worry about it. Stay naked. I'm dying for a bath." I'm a little stressed. For the past week, we've spoken on the phone every night before going to sleep and he told me several times we should stop seeing each other. I defused the situation each time, saying things such as my cat was jumping on the door frame or an ambulance was going by the apartment drowning out the sound of his voice. I'm scared. I don't want him telling me tonight that he doesn't want to see me anymore. It might be selfish but I like sharing myself between Samuel and Alain, like in the Brigitte Bardot song *Ciel de lit.* I have a lover for sex and a husband for life.

He tells me he hasn't found any furniture to suit his taste

in the antique shops on Notre Dame Street but he got me a rose and a small painted ceramic tile, "halfway between a bad Picasso, Chagall, or Matisse sketch." He shows it to me and starts drawing my bath. He makes some martinis and spills some into the neckline of my dress. Pulling on the fabric, he takes my breasts out and licks them. I undress and he leaves me to put on some music. He tells me he chose an old song by a punk-alternative German band called Sprung aus den Wolken. I suspect he's already drunk, laughing and singing too loudly.

He asks me how my day went. I tell him my mother phoned me a few minutes before I had to go meet him, "One of their neighbors, the brother of my best friend when I was a kid, was featured in a magazine article this month, recounting how he saved a half-unconscious policewoman, but my mom's put off because he's just been sent to detox. He had sold his winter boots to buy some coke and had committed armed robbery at the grocery store where he used to work. The cashier recognized his voice and shoes and he was arrested by the same policewoman he had saved." Alain sympathizes, his best friend when he lived in Paris was also addicted to hard drugs. I splash some water on him to lighten the mood and tell him how my mom's not sure if she should let one of my brothers, the one that didn't go to Katimavik, invite a girl to sleep over at the house. "You know what she calls the girl? She says his 'fuck girl' instead of 'fuck friend'! I found her too funny trying to use the same vocabulary as my brothers but failing miserably. I was laughing so hard. I think my mother must now think I'm as high as my former best friend's brother because I kept laughing without telling her why."

Alain takes my face in his hands and kisses me. "I think about you too often, I think. Yesterday I partied with some friends in Old Montreal and kept thinking of you. I danced and couldn't wait to come home, a bit drunk, to check if you had sent me an email. I love you." He sees that I'm shocked and a bit panicked. "You don't have to say it back." I start to cry, and reveal I'm married. "I can't tell you I love you, that wouldn't be fair, I don't know what to think, I never thought it'd turn out this way between us, and I never thought I'd want to leave Samuel one day." Alain laughs. "Want to tell me about Samuel? I know two and they're both gay. They always make me skip the lineup when I go to their clubs. I'm also with someone at the moment but it's not as serious as you and Samuel I guess. Actually she's with me. She's pretty, nice and young. But I don't want to be with her. She wanted it so much, she decided we'd be together. I like making her come but each time I do, I think of you."

We part ways the next morning after he's fucked me on the kitchen counter next to the Breville coffeemaker. Before going to work, I have to pick up the Tinker Bell costume that I reserved for Halloween. Alain notices some self-tanning lotion stains on the collar of my coat and lends me a Peruvian hat. It's snowing outside, it's so pretty, the first snow of the fall. I kiss him and tell him not to throw the rose away, even when it becomes dry and wrinkled, I want to do the same as Marguerite Duras who kept flowers, even dried ones, in her house indefinitely.

I stop at the grocery store near the agency and buy some shampoo and conditioner. I wash my hair and apply a Bella Pella facial clay mask I leave on for ten minutes before washing my face under cold running water and applying makeup. I'm fresh-faced when I call Debbie to let her know I'm ready to see my first client before 9:30 A.M. The Concordia professor comes to see me, booking two hours, and hands me a $50 Chapters gift certificate. "I find it more personal than cash as a tip." I thank him and he asks me to put some bottles of water and orange juice in the fridge. He also brought some granola bars to share in between lovemaking sessions. After making me climax twice, he reassures me about school. "All the professors prefer students that don't get straight A's, overachievers are not interesting, they're not the ones I prefer mentoring into doing a master's." I then entertain a native man so obese I can only blow his tiny penis hidden between two folds of flesh.

I don't have another client for the rest of the day and ask Debbie who's working in apartment 708. She says it should have been Amy but she walked out in the middle of her shift yesterday. "She left with all the money but left a black dress behind. If it fits you, you can have it. It's hanging in the living room closet. You're the only girl working today. It's pretty dead. I had to say no to a client while you were with your first one. It's cold outside, maybe the guys prefer staying in their office on their lunch hour today, maybe it'll get busier tonight." I would have liked to make more money today. I wanted to get Porcelaine a collar adorned with Swarovski crystals and, at the risk of suffering from mercury poisoning, buy $30 worth of sushi every day of November.

A thirty-something man with a bad stubble arrives ten minutes before 5 P.M. I let him in and he tells me his girlfriend just dumped him. "We had been together for five years. She told me I was a lousy lay. I need to know what to do to give a woman pleasure. I want you to show me everything." I enthusiastically show him all my favorite positions, telling him, "guys like girls on top. I don't. Don't ask you next girlfriend to do that on the first night, she'll get bored." I go down on all fours and ask him to come behind me and penetrate me. "I love this, it feels great, I can really feel you deep inside my pussy. Can you feel my tight cunt?" He keeps a straight face as if he's taking mental notes, as if he had only vanilla sex for the last five years with his former girlfriend. Before he can climax, I push him away, kneeling down on the bed, and order him to go down on me and nibble on my tits. He applies himself, giving me timid looks from time to time. I lower his head so he can lick my clit. I recommend that he wet one or two fingers and insert them into my pussy. I need more than just tongue to climax, I need to be full.

Two days later, after a busier day in Dorval, I come back to my apartment with greasy hair, a red face, and a sore pussy. I wash and change into my Tinker Bell costume for the Halloween party my cousin organized in an abandoned factory close to her place. I invite Samuel to join me but he's tired and says he'll go to bed early after baking some Rice Krispies squares. I call Alain to ask him if he gave candy to the neighborhood children but he doesn't pick up. I decide to write him an email, then notice he wrote me a short humorless one. "We should go back to a more basic relationship, without hopes and dreams. That way, I won't annoy you with my old fart feelings. We'll use condoms. I'll come see you at the agency and call you Marissa. I'm not Samuel. I could never accept sharing the woman I love with others. Maybe I'm too Latin. Or maybe I just don't want my pride to get hurt. Whatever the reason, it's better this way."

I put some silver shadow on my eyelids to think about something else and refrain from crying. I kiss Samuel, vowing never to be vulnerable again, to be Marissa for everybody, to never be sad, to be strong and smile only with the cold smile of an angel, to take advantage of everything, like Alain's dick and money, and never leave any long black hair in his condo, on his pillows, or in his tub.

I follow the directions on the abandoned factory walls and climb up the steps, too scared I might get stuck in the elevator, and end up in a big artist studio with about a hundred people. Porn films are playing on giant screens. I'm dizzy, it's all so pretty. I'm strong and show that cold angel smile, but I don't know anyone here. I look for my cousin who's usually easy to spot with her platinum blond hair. I stay two hours on the dance floor, letting boys and girls rub against my back. As soon as they try putting their fingers inside me, I leave the dance floor, drink vodka from the flask of a girl dressed up as Marilyn Monroe, and leave the party. I don't want to bump into people on the street, or clients from the twenty-four-hour pizza parlor or the pool room which is still open. I hail a taxi and through its dirty window observe the city that's way more lively than I am.

I drink a latte full of chocolate shavings while waiting for my hairdresser at the Pure hair salon to cut my dead ends. He's busy with another client, applying toner on her hair. She just came from another salon, her hair more yellow than blonde. I think my hairdresser's great. He's reassuring and funny, and makes the best lattes. He asks me if I vacationed anywhere lately. I give him the name of my self-tanning lotion and thank him as I leave to go shopping at the upscale Cours Mont-Royal mall. I want to buy Samuel a leather jacket and a couple of scarves. I also stop in a video rental store, hoping to find a useful film for my final paper for Quebec Cinema, one of the classes I'm taking this semester. I chose to write about the male persona in Quebec cinema and how it seems to be afflicted by the Peter Pan Syndrome. I choose André Turpin's *Soft Shell Man,* which tells the story of a photographer who obsessively wants to seduce. He tries to please everyone, while being a compulsive liar, never questioning his futile motivations.

I stop at Ripaille et Bombance and I'm at the checkout paying for a moose meat pie and a black chocolate pudding when I feel my cell phone vibrating in my Moto-brand jeans pocket. I recognize Alain's nonchalant voice. "Parting ways now would have been romantic, don't you think? But I love being completely mad about you. How are you? Want to come see me soon?" Without thinking twice about it, I tell him I can come over tonight. He accepts. I think this makes him happy, and I get changed at the apartment, hoping the products used by my hairdresser won't offend Alain's delicate sense of smell. I leave the prepared meals in the fridge and pin a note on the bulletin board warning Samuel I'll be home around midnight and saying I left new clothes for him on the bed.

I bump into Alain's neighbors walking their Dachshund and Golden Retriever dogs. Alain asks me if I've ever had cod *brandade* and I say I haven't. He invites me to take a seat in front of him while he cooks and again gives me the copy of *One Hundred Years of Solitude*. "I used one of your hairs as a bookmark." I smile. "That's nice of you to think of me like that. I think of you too, even at work, which makes it odd at times. Oh, you'll see I've hurt myself. I almost lost a toe. I'm in the bathroom at the agency when I hear my cell phone ringing. I drop my brush on my lip balm, the one that's watermelon-flavored. It falls in the toilet. I'm super sad but I have to run to answer the call as a client's just arrived. And I run into a floor joint, hurting my toe, making it bleed, and I'm screaming like a banshee in front of the new client, who looks like he doesn't know what to think of me."

Alain laughs and asks to see my toe. I refuse, saying it's too scary looking. He tries to take off my pantyhose. I struggle while playfully screaming. He holds my wrists tightly. "Wednesday night, I came home with Juliette and I had fun trying to hide your pink panties under the bed. Naughty girl, did you forget them or leave them here on purpose? And on Thursday, Joanie wanted to sleep over but I was too tired. Oh, and there's also Rebecca whom I'm seeing, a beautiful Bosnian girl who dreams of starting a big family, and Léonie too, who's even more beautiful but fortunately doesn't have any dreams. I'd like to be with you one day, but I have expectations, I'm sorry, I have no right to. If I'm with you, I don't want to make other women come and I don't want you to work, so that's why I think it's a better idea not to be together." He lets go of my wrists and I stare at him with an open mouth, not knowing what to say. "I wish I could have met your daughter and seen all the little ducks she brings with her in the bath tub."

Alain sighs. "Brat." I say that, despite still being attached to Samuel, I'd be ready to leave him to the memories of what we used to be and the dreams we shared that will never come true. It's sad. I really believed we'd live happily ever after, and own a wooden house in the countryside complete with rocking chairs on the front porch. I'd drink green tea, my face all creased, with a thousand abandoned cats in my wooden house and canaries in the garden. But I can't imagine not working at the agency, just like that, without a safety net, just so I could fully live a love story that might last only a couple of months. I want to be independent, I need my independence. I want to rely only on myself and never ask anyone for money, even the guy with whom I'd be sharing a condo. "I can't picture myself quitting. I'd do it, but only because I know you wouldn't accept it. Maybe I could work only one day a week. I really like the relationship I have with my clients, I like that they leave my company happy, I like bettering my English by talking to Anglophones. And I shop too much, I'm addicted to it all, the clothes, the celebrity gossip, and I know you'll say I'm making up useless needs and that money shouldn't be the key issue, I know it's ridiculous but I can't picture myself doing any other type of work. I'm lazy, too busy with school and not intelligent enough. I only know how to smile, fuck, and talk about literary counterculture. I'd like to be less superficial. I didn't use to be like that."

Alain shakes his head and tells me to lie down on the

wooden floor. He raises each of my legs, one by one, to take off my pantyhose. He also takes off my dress, sliding it over my head. He penetrates me without saying a word, without spitting in his hand first, and I don't know if I should look at him. I stroke his chest hair and his back and regret not having asked him to make a fire in the fireplace instead of saying too much.

# Golden Ballerina Shoes in the Snow and Dried Sperm in my Hair

On November 18, I wake up happy, eat half a banana-nut muffin, fill my Lululemon gym bag, and check my emails. I read a message Alain sent me five hours ago, without making sense of it. "I understand about Samuel. I don't understand about work. Money is never, should never be an issue. Do you believe I wouldn't have provided for everything? Keep your clients. Love them. I never want to hear the sound of your voice again. I'm going to wash away every trace of you, every dream, every illusion I had. Tomorrow, I'll be inside another woman. Thanks for letting me go, it's better that way. Go back to being who you've always been. Be happy. Forgive me for having had expectations. I don't feel a thing for you, not even anger, nothing at all, except contempt."

My crying wakes Samuel. I scream and collapse on the floor, I have lower abdominal pain, and I can't move. I lie down on my back. I'm in pain for several minutes. I'd like to call Alain, to be reassured, so he can tell me all is well but I don't, knowing he wouldn't pick up and I'd feel even more pathetic, lying down by the door, my head on my Lululemon gym bag, my hand on my cell phone, listening to his answering machine message, without any voice telling me this too shall pass. I get up. Samuel's dumbfounded. I tell him to go back to bed and I try to breathe normally and stop crying. I don't want to have a swollen face for my clients. I look online for the Website of the company Alain works for, write down the phone number, and leave without knowing if I'll survive the day. I feel faint at every street corner. I just want to sit still on a subway train with an empty gaze and forget I deserve the contempt of the man I love more than I thought, forget I'm a slut who thinks she's a nice girl, forget how the trade I chose to earn money makes me distance myself from everyone except those who stay thirty minutes or an hour between my legs.

The apartment keys are not under the fire alarm in their magnetic hiding place. I knock at Brandon's apartment. He opens the door and I see Hélène showing him her Nicaragua pictures. She volunteers at least two months a year in Third World countries. She says she's exhausted. She worked until 1 A.M. the previous night with an office tower cleaning crew. She and Anna are the only two escorts I know who care to have a legal job. Once inside apartment 408, I rush to call Alain, who doesn't pick up. I leave him a message and get dressed. I'm a robot in front of the mirror and I turn the volume of the TV very high, not caring neighbors might complain. I watch music videos and leave him another message: "I'm working at the agency today. Please come and I'll leave with you." I call him back: "You said the opposite the other day, basking in sunlight, staring at the bill for your fucking mattress, you said I was important to you, but I was just another girl, a passing fancy, I find it hard having just been another girl to you, I thought I was more than that."

My first client arrives, my heart's pounding. I look through the peephole and I don't see Alain, but an overly tanned guy. He's nice, he brought me sweet almond massage oil. I lie down and close my eyes. He's very good. He says I'm tense. "You should massage yourself at home, you can use tennis balls, lie on top of them or put some against a wall and let them roll against your back." He nicknames me "the nymph" and fucks me with his tiny one-inch-long-when-hard penis. I can't feel a thing. I force myself to look at him, thinking of Alain's gray eyes and all the women he promised to fuck, and I picture them all prettier, without a red nose or overwaxed eyebrows, more interesting, less shy, and I see them dancing with him and singing and tasting his Béchamel sauce with a spoon. I'm sure they can all be happy, those girls, without having to hide envelopes inside sugary cereal boxes.

The hippie sailor comes to see me next. He'll soon be back on his boat for three months, this time going to Brazil. I let him take a picture of me with his cell phone, sitting on the bed with my legs straightened, and I smile, waiting for him to get a satisfying shot. He penetrates me after I've poured a ton of lubricant on his dick and between my legs. I firmly clutch a pillow. I don't know if I'll be able to do this all day. He leaves after giving me a copy of *Siddhartha*, by his favorite author, Hermann Hesse. I had told him I hadn't read it. I kiss his sunburned skin that's seen many different shores and thank him. His thoughtfulness touches me. I call Alain's office and give his secretary a fake name. She transfers me right away. When he recognizes my voice he tells me to stop calling and hangs up. This breaks my heart, again. I want to throw my cell phone against the wall and look at all the broken pieces lying around the room for hours.

My next client, David, a businessman from Beaconsfield[22] whose pants don't match his jacket books an hour with me. "It's hard to resist you," he says, and when he climaxes after twenty minutes he asks me if he can go see Hélène without having to pay extra. I tell him no. I don't understand how some clients can surmise we'd give ourselves to them at a

---

22. West Island town, just west of Montreal

discount, thinking we're paid too much. Some say grocery store cashiers should be pretty and have manicured hands; others thank us for accepting them, thank us for existing, and are willing to pay much more than $200 for an orgasm. Maybe I should travel for a while, and listen to more Christina Aguilera despite Samuel not being able to stand her.

Colin, the comic book artist, schedules an hour with me and asks me what my real name is. I tell him. He says it'll soon be his birthday and I write the date in my Paperblanks notebook. He adds, while playing with his faded shirt buttons, that he'd like to see me outside of the agency, not to fuck but just to talk and show me his favorite café and see me in my everyday clothes and not in my too-short skirt with my too-tight tank top. He says that sometimes when he gets back home, he finds sequins on his clothes and collects them. I tell him softly I don't have time to see clients outside of work. The Concordia professor brings me a huge bouquet of flowers and tastes his cum from the condom after having climaxed.

I'm so busy I manage not to think about Alain and to fuck an old guy who has trouble getting a hard-on and who lets me know he's bored now that the first snow took golf away from him. Tony comes see me in the middle of the afternoon and I jump into his arms, telling him he's lost more weight. He's very proud. "One of my old friends from when I was fifteen plays football and has decided to help me train." He says he ate at ChuChai, a vegetarian restaurant on St. Denis Street with a colleague of his who looks a bit like me. "I miss you. Talking with her made me think of you." He orgasms with his tongue sticking out while caressing my clit. When he gets dressed, he puts his underwear on inside out. Samir follows him in and I accidentally call him Alain. I'm very embarrassed and turn bright red while apologizing, but Samir, who's a gentleman, tells me he's ready to forgive my absentmindedness. A Sikh Indian man, who looks like Freddy Prinze Jr. but skinnier, is my last client. I love him. He came to see me twice in one day in Dorval. He's very gentle and relaxes me. He lets me touch the pendant around his neck so it'll bring me strength.

I leave while congratulating Sophie on the purchase of her house, under her mother's name, and call my cousin Cheryl. I feel like Carrie Bradshaw, the lead character in *Sex and the City*, only sluttier. I hail a cab, my miniskirt showing my butt crease, and I almost drop the bouquet of flowers, my arms full with my Lululemon gym bag full of makeup and $50 bills. I crash in the back seat of the taxi, giving him my address while talking to my cousin on the phone. "Alain hates me. He doesn't want to see me again, ever. I don't know what to do. I called him all day in between clients, it was hell! Tell me you don't have any plans tonight and want to get drunk with me."

I wear the same dress I had on at work. I don't know or care if it smells of latex, cum, or sweat. I put on my summer golden ballerina shoes and thank Samuel for making celery and broccoli soup. "I'm not really hungry, but I want to try it. Could you heat up just a spoonful for me?" Then I meet up with my cousin in a jazz bar I'd never been to before called The Bebop. When I arrive, my cousin's already there and we're the only clients. We sit at a remote table made of dark wood and I order green apple martinis for both of us. I show her a copy of Alain's email. "Does he start every relationship just to forget the previous one? Then when it's over, he finds another girl just like that, to start fresh, over and over again? It's not fair, Cheryl. I know I'm being horrible to Samuel, I feel like beating him sometimes because I don't know how to love him right, but I never suspected I'd feel this way. I should never have agreed to see him, I should never have believed all he did for me was true and without malice. Why did he go down on me, why? So he can brag that he made a whore come? And when he told me he loved me, what did it mean? I waited for him all day and he never came."

I tell her I feel like taking a trip and say she should come with me. We could go to the Dominican Republic and fuck lots of Latinos. She plays with a strand of her hair and says, "Remember when we went to see our grandparents in Florida together? We had bought lots of happy face earrings. I got my earlobes pierced for the third time. Was it you or me that bought that love potion?" I interrupt her. "And I kept wanting to watch that show with Carmen Electra on MTV! We read *Reader's Digest* for hours and magazines with Jonathan Taylor Thomas on the cover! We had watched so many *X-Files* episodes we woke our grandparents one night, sure aliens were outside our bedroom window!" Cheryl hits the table "There were aliens!"

My cousin tells me Nathalie's now an escort in the US. "She left for New York City. She thinks she'll get to be in hip hop music videos or become some sculptor's muse. She's in love with a girl who sells cupcakes and goes out every night. She lets me use her studio, the one where she painted and did taxidermy." I ask her how it's going with Miguel and Francis. She says Francis had started sleeping with her female roommate again, but has stopped. She doesn't give a damn, he can't get hard anymore and she doesn't know why, it drives her nuts. "I asked to borrow $200 from my dad and spent it all on La Senza lingerie."

When she goes off to the downstairs bathroom, I can't help but pick up my cell phone and try to reach Alain. He answers and speaks in a tired voice when I ask him all my questions. He simply says I hurt him and I apologize for the loud music. I'm shocked. I never thought I'd hurt him. I thought making me listen to the old punk records he listened to while hitchhiking through England in order to attend these bands' concerts made him happy. I thought talking to me about his lawyers who were supposedly taking care of his divorce made him happy. I didn't think I could hurt someone without meaning to. My cousin returns, but looks away while I talk on the phone. I thought maybe I would go see Alain after our drinks, but by the sound of his voice I understand he'd reject me, even if I cried, even if I said I was sorry. It wouldn't be enough. I look at my reflection in my Anna Taintor pocket mirror. I'm not crying, my cheeks are still pink with powdered blush, and my eyes are shiny, thanks to the apple green eyeliner I applied. A Bebop patron buys us another martini. My cousin isn't embarrassed to ignore him after having thanked him. She tells me her mom's out of the psychiatric hospital and back at home. She has to see a psychologist once a week and take her meds. "I went to see her and on her fridge, covered in magnetic words, she had emphasized the words *madness, mad* and *lost*. I didn't tell her I had noticed."

We leave the bar, walk along St. Denis Street, and go through the St. Louis Square I used to cross when I went to Alex's, the photographer. We stop at a fast food joint to eat some onion rings and a cheeseburger. She leaves in a taxi cab and I walk home, the falling snow soaking my ballerina shoes, which will be too wet and too damaged to wear again. I walk and look at store displays, unable to stop myself from taking mental notes of the ones that have gorgeous dresses on sale. Once I reach the apartment, I'm surprised that I don't collapse. I take a hot shower without turning on any lights, looking for dried sperm in my hair, or the perfumed smell of the bar, or my cousin, or onion rings, or other men.

For three days I eat nothing but pears. They're delicious in November. I don't have enough appetite to bite into anything else. I don't call my parents back and they leave worried messages on my answering machine. We usually speak every day or so. I refuse to tell Samuel anything, just give him more money for weed. Two other clients ask me why I'm an escort, as Alain did, not understanding why. They say I'm intelligent, pretty, and normal. A girl-next-door type like me shouldn't be working in that industry. I don't know why I'm doing it anymore. I re-read Alain's breakup email without crying, and his last email as well where he wrote that he had a house-warming party at his condo and had invited lots of women, three for each guy present. He wrote that he still had lots of Champagne bottles to drink and told me he was finishing one off while smelling Joanie's pussy on his fingers.

I start reading another David Sedaris book. He makes me laugh a lot. He was just hired as a Santa Claus village elf and has just heard that a group of deaf children are about to visit. I sometimes forget to think about Alain, about the possibility of having been loved by a man who found me beautiful despite the white spots on my back and the blisters on my feet and the black hair I leave everywhere. I forget to think about the fact that I no longer love Samuel, that I love nothing anymore, except for all the high-heeled shoes I've accumulated in my closet, when I read, "My sister Amy lives above a deaf girl and has learned quite a bit of sign language. She taught some to me and so now I am able to say, 'Santa has a tumor in his head the size of an olive. Maybe it will go away tomorrow but I don't think so.'"

# If You Were an Escort, Would You Be a Girlfriend Experience (GFE), a Porn Star Experience (PSE), or a Little Slut Who'd Quit After Two Weeks?

1. Would you be comfortable enough to kiss strangers with mouths thinner than your stepmother's mustache?

    a) Yes, it'd bring me closer to my clients and I'd feel more like their girlfriend than their whore.
    b) I wouldn't really get a chance to kiss them, once sitting on their dick with my back to them.
    c) Only if the client looks like my best friend's dad. And with a $50 tip.


2. Do you go to the gym?

    a) I swim twice a week.
    b) Every night. I work out for at least an hour. I do weights and cardio. I want a nice round black girl's ass, and abs like those the bikini girls on the cover of Sports Illustrated have, and Madonna's biceps.
    c) I do Pilates with my best friend once every two weeks in a Zen studio. Gyms smell too bad.


3. What's your hair color?

    a) Brown.
    b) Platinum blond with hair extensions.
    c) Red with blond streaks like my neighbor, my cousin, and the cashier at the grocery store.

4. What do you do after someone paid you for sex?

   a) I hug them.
   b) I take a shower.
   c) I look to see how badly I need a manicure.


5. What do you say to a client who invites you for an evening of movies and chocolate fondue?

   a) "Oh, that's so sweet, maybe one day, but I'm too busy this week walking the dog for my neighbor who has a cold, and I have 10,000 homeworks to do for school."
   b) "What? You want to watch me do something other than get down on all fours for you?"
   c) "I never go to the movies and I'm allergic to chocolate, plus I'd never go out with guys as old as my best friend's dad."

# Results

If you have more A's, you're an authentic GFE (Girlfriend Experience) and you have a bleeding heart like Elisabeth Shue in Leaving Las Vegas, ready to accompany a nice client on his descent through alcoholism. Not only are you sexy, you also can name great Brazilian film directors and the best Port wines, and clients can picture you wearing plaid pajamas, with messy hair, minus any makeup, eating nachos in front of the TV.

If you have more B's, you're an impressive PSE (Porn Star Experience). You're probably very flexible thanks to all those gymnastics classes you took when you were a child, you can do a hundred different sex positions in an hour, and your makeup is worthy of a Lise Watier advertisement. On the other hand, you don't talk to your clients, you only scream.

If you have more C's, you're not meant to work in the sex industry. You're a slut who plays the escort all through November and December just to be able to afford more Christmas gifts. You then quit and will see your best friend's therapist for ten years.

# A Twenty-First Century Pretty Woman Who Eats Froot Loops in Bed

My dad has been writing me emails. He sends me pictures of Minus and Holden Caulfield, whose tail sometimes ends up in my mother's coffee. He says he loves me and writes things like "my little girl" or "my beautiful Mélodie." I'm very touched. At first, I did not reciprocate to his endearing notes, but now I'm adding almost timidly that I love him too in my emails.

I would like to go see them for a few days. I don't know what will become of me if I keep lying to my family and ignoring Samuel. I think about Alain all the time, doing my grocery shopping, staring at the corn flour which reminds me of his polenta and his cooking, and I think about his tattoo each time I see an ad about reptiles. Every time I go by the St. Henri metro station, I think of his condo, so close and yet so far, and when I read the newspaper, I think of him, bringing me the paper in bed once with croissants and strawberry Danishes. I only read one section before awkwardly folding it and putting it on the bedside table. I buy Samuel some Clinique Happy perfume, so I'll smell another man on his neck, and agree to follow an Italian client named Dino to one of his friends' house in Hampstead[23] to become even sluttier and prove I was right in believing I don't deserve a man's

---

23. Small town on the island of Montreal

love.

I wait for Dino at the Namur metro station. In his car, he keeps saying his friend Mario has a big dick and I'll love him. His friend shows me around his house, telling me it cost a fortune, as if I were a poor little girl from the ghetto who dreams of being like Julia Roberts in *Pretty Woman* and find a client to make her believe she's a princess in a fairy tale, have elocution lessons, and learn all about table etiquette. Mario gives me a chocolate chip cookie. "My wife baked them yesterday." The guys don't compliment me on my velvet dress, just like the one Madonna wore recently at an award ceremony. In Mario's room, I see a portrait of his wife and their two kids. I ask them to pay me right away and Dino dares debate with me how much he owes. I tell him calmly I'm ready to leave right now if he doesn't give me the $400 we had agreed upon beforehand. The two friends exchange glances before giving me the money. I don't count it and take off my dress. Mario tells Dino he should put it in my ass, not talking to me directly. I feel as lost as Brenda in *Six Feet Under*. I kneel down on the flowery bedspread as Dino slips inside my ass. He's sure he has a big dick and is proud of it, but actually it's tiny, so I don't care that he's putting it into my tightest hole. Mario plays with himself while watching us, and Dino whispers in my ear to take a good look at his friend's cock, "Do you like it? It's big, isn't it, and you can't wait to have it inside you, can you? Slut." He seems to me he likes it a little too much. I blow Mario, who slaps me. I don't put up any resistance and Dino climaxes in my ass before Mario had a chance to slide into my pussy.

I continue to blow Mario who wants to fuck my ass next. "I have a lover who never wanted me to sodomize her until one night I got her drunk on daiquiris and she agreed. Now she always wants me to fuck her that way. She doesn't even want my dick in her pussy, only in her ass." I refuse unless he pays $100 more. I feel pathetic. Dino comes out of the bathroom and gets dressed while I try to get Mario's cock harder. Dino apologizes, "I won't be able to get another hard-on for at least an hour now that I've come, but you two have fun, I'll go have some chocolate chip cookies. The bedroom wallpaper's really nice, was it you or your wife who chose it?" As Mario penetrates me, a cell phone starts vibrating in his pants pocket on the floor. Panicked, he tells me to be quiet and answers, "I'm at home. I had forgotten a client file. I love you, honey."

He hangs up. I stare at my nails painted with OPI's Little Red Wagon nail polish, raise my head, and go back down on all fours so he can fuck me. "You smell like peaches." I play with his balls, wanting him to empty his sack as soon as possible so I can get back into Dino's car and go to class where I can ask the other students if my velvet dress suits me and if I need Botox injections. I feel disgusting. I can't wait to go to the bathroom and check if Dino's condom is full of shit or not, wash my ass and pussy, and fill my mouth with mint-flavored toothpaste.

In Dino's Audi, I already know I'm going to stop working. I get a call, it's Fabrice. I tell him I'll call him back later, "Hey, I'm working, dirty boy." I go to class, hand the professor my paper on the Peter Pan syndrome afflicting male characters in modern Quebec cinema, and leave, stepping on my velvet dress. I call Alain and say, "I love you." It's my first time telling him for real. I wait for his reaction. He answers after a long silence, "You know I do too. I'm not ready to see you. I'm going to a private club for work, then having drinks with a friend. I'll call you tomorrow."

Shaking with uncertainty, I enter the apartment where Samuel's listening to Boards of Canada. He asks me if I want to play a game of Scrabble. Without thinking I tell him I no longer want to be with him. "I'll continue paying for the apartment. I'm sorry. I'd like to keep on having breakfast at Cora's and watching *Desperate Housewives* episodes here with you but I just want to be alone." Samuel doesn't understand, and he cries. We remain in each other's arms a long while, then I order some take-out. We share a seafood pizza and he keeps telling me he doesn't believe me. I want to run away and book a hotel room, but we fall asleep with the three cats between us.

I forget to pay my cell phone bill, not wanting to reach anyone, and stay at home trying to do advanced yoga positions when I receive an email from Alain. He says he's tried to reach me over the phone for the last two days, and he's ready to have me all to himself, despite my anxieties, my clumsiness, and my threats to cut my wrists with a razor blade if we disagree about anything. "I can't stand being without you. You're not like the others, if that's what you fear. Please don't let me lose you. I want to introduce you to my daughter. I love you because you love Duras and I can't stand her. Because you cry in my arms. Because you're kind of lost. Because you love the snow. I also love you because being with you will allow me to be me, and being myself won't burden you. I love you because with you I can rest, and I love that you caused me this much pain. I love you because my liver hurts. The Romans, well, the original ones, before Jesus came, the Romans thought the liver was the seat of love. To be fair, with all they used to drink during their orgies, they must have had bad liver pangs they could have mistaken for broken hearts. I'm going boozing tonight, I miss you too much. Don't force me to have to wash all trace of you away. I don't want to hear of it. I want you to have the courage to come join me. I'll welcome you with open arms. I hope you'll come see me soon. I want you to decide. Tomorrow they'll deliver my new mattresses and I want you to be the only one to try them out."

I jump into a cab with two garbage bags full of clothes.

I'm very nervous as I head towards Alain's place, thinking this is all happening very fast. He's waiting for me in the stairwell and takes me into his arms. He forgets to help me with my big bags as he opens the door of his condo. We fuck in front of his fireplace as they do in bad porn films. I move into his apartment, bringing more and more garbage bags full of my previous life, the bracelets I bought in California, my coconut-scented soap, my makeup, my books, and leave Samuel with everything else, the big screen TV, the martini glasses, my escort miniskirts I never want to wear again, the living room table the Morphée shop has just delivered, my condoms, the cats, and the rat. It breaks my heart but I don't want Samuel to feel abandoned by them as well. I also leave behind my stuffed animals, my dawn simulator, the tickets for Sarah Kane's *4.48 Psychosis*, the kitsch paintings bought at Urban Outfitters. I don't want to bring any of this with me until I feel as if I have a home elsewhere. I also leave my notebooks behind and drop out of all my classes, except my contemporary dance class.

In the morning, I stay in bed and listen to Alain listen to Coldplay while fixing his coffee. Around noon I eat Froot Loops in bed while leafing through the newspaper *La Presse*, wondering if I did the right thing dropping everything for a *Pretty Woman* love story, but without the limousine and the millions of dollars, for a guy who wakes me up five times a night to fuck and continually says he loves me while yelling at me when I don't wash a glass correctly. I don't know how to be with Alain. I just went from being his whore to being his girlfriend. I don't know if I'm supposed to wait for him to get home while cleaning the place dressed like Snow White, throwing away the waxing strips he uses on his back, and cooking a meal for him, or wait on all fours on the carpet in the hallway with geisha balls that have been vibrating inside my pussy since early afternoon. I don't feel useful, unless I spread my legs. I never used to do much around the apartment. Samuel cooked and never criticized me if my books or panties were lying around the floor or piling up on top of a chest of drawers, never asked me to scrub the bath tub on a daily basis, and I only swallowed his cum once every two months.

I eat some clementines and listen to Elliott Smith, Keren Ann, or NIN, "What have I become / My sweetest friend / Everyone I know goes away / In the end / And you could have it all / My empire of dirt / I will let you down / I will make you hurt", sitting on the floor, huddled next to the heating vent, looking at the Lachine Canal. Debbie calls me wondering if I'm really sure I don't want to come back and work for her. "I liked your previous boyfriend better. Why did you break up?" I read the comments left by my clients on the MERB Website over and over again and I smile, happy I mattered to them,

"I miss her and I pray she'll come back."

"Marissa was great, I miss her very much (has anyone heard from her?)."

"I agree with everyone, Marissa was the best girl that agency ever had."

I continue to lose weight because I know Alain likes it when I'm lying on my back and he can see all my ribs as I arch my back while climaxing. I call Samuel and can tell by his tone of voice he's still sad and wants me back even though I was mean and unfair to him, "I wake up in the morning and it takes me a while to remember you're gone. Gontran keeps on escaping from his cage, I don't know how, and today he hid in a box of granola bars. The cats were super scared and hid underneath the living room couch for a long time."

It's Friday and I'm shopping at Marciano to buy sexier dresses than the ones worn by the barmaids with big boobs that Alain used to bring home to fuck at 4 A.M. while drunk on the bed where I used to leave long black hairs. I return with a bag full of tight dresses *à la* Roland Mouret, red low-necked sweaters, and necklaces with golden pendants. I can hear laughter on the other side of his apartment door and remember his two-year-old daughter is spending the weekend with him, which I had forgotten. I suddenly feel very nervous wondering if she'll like me, if I'll like her, if I'll have to change her diapers, and if she still sleeps in the same bed as her dad. I'm terrified, wondering if I'm really capable of being with a man who'll never see me as the most important person in the world.

I enter, and as soon as the little girl sees me, she opens her arms to hug me. I hug her back, my eyes tearing up from the easiness of it and because she seems to like me already. I show Alain my purchases and she reaches to grab my necklaces. I let her have them, though fearing she might break them by pulling too hard on the delicate chains, but I want to seem like a nice stepmother. Alain watches a Barney the Dinosaur show with her and makes her burst into laughter by tickling her with her plush toys, and I think about Porcelaine and how I'd like to hold her in my arms right now. The little girl wakes up at 3 A.M., slams our bedroom door against the wall, and reaches out for her dad to pick her up and put her between us. She brings her toys to bed and keeps on kicking me. I pretend I'm sleeping but can't believe I'll have to spend the whole weekend barely sleeping, getting a small fire truck rolled on my ass. I went from an escort who got hour-long massages from her clients to a stepmother with horrible rings under my eyes who finds it cute but scary to be leaning all the Barney songs by heart.

I decide to go out on Saturday night and meet up with Molly at the Sainte-Élisabeth Pub, a Latin Quarter bar, very popular among students. I tell her I left Samuel and that she'd probably like Alain despite the fact he doesn't spend all his evenings smoking joint after joint. She seems surprised and pouts like a spoiled brat. "I guess we'll never do a foursome with our guys! How's Alain? Does he fuck you better? Is he a perv? What does he do for a living?" I tell her I'd like her to meet Alain. "I'd like to know what you think of him. He's so different from Samuel. And he knows how to fuck me, I swear I'll never go back to men under thirty-five. I'm not sure what he does for a living, I don't understand a thing about business and IT, my brain can't grasp any of it. He does product repositioning so they'll penetrate the market successfully. Some kind of creative marketing I think."

We down our vodka-cranberries. Molly takes off her sneakers and tries on my high heel shoes. She walks like a wannabe model in the bar and falls into my arms. "Hey, you're not wearing a bra either. I want to touch your boobs, can I?" She opens my dress, takes hold of my breasts. "They're pretty! Bigger than mine!" I don't believe her so I raise her shirt. "Yours are pointier!" I kiss them. As a barman approaches, I take Molly's hand and tell her we should go into the bathroom before the barman kicks us out. We get into the bathroom, as giddy as drunk schoolgirls, and look at our breasts in the mirror. I ask her to bite my nipples and she refuses, licking them instead, and caressing them while sounding like a bitch in heat. I unzip her pants and lower them. I want to see her pussy and smell it. She's trimmed down there and I kiss and suck on her clit. After a few minutes, I get bored, lean against the mirror, and ask her to taste me too. She puts a finger inside me and tells me I'm really soft. She turns me on but I know I won't be able to come standing up, trying to keep my balance on my high heels. We kiss and leave the bathroom to order more vodka-cranberries.

I tell her I can still smell her pussy, putting my face against her breasts, half lying down on the Sainte-Élisabeth Pub leather couch. I notice it's almost 2 A.M. "Oh fuck,

Alain's daughter will wake up in three hours tops, I'll be a zombie tomorrow." Molly scowls at me, "He has a daughter? I went on a trip two years ago with my sister-in-law and her daughter, I was super happy at first but it became annoying in no time, I thought kids were like dogs, you know, but forget it, my sister-in-law didn't even have any fun, her daughter required all her attention." I think comparing her niece to an animal is stupid, but I laugh and tell her at least I know how to change diapers and put bows in Alain's daughter's thin blond hair. I find a convenience store in which I buy a *pain au chocolat* because I'm starving, then take a cab. At the condo, I spill the contents of my purse while looking for my keys and empty my stomach on the hallway carpet. I'm too dizzy to suspect Alain won't be too happy to wake up next to a girl smelling of Givenchy perfume, musky pussy juice, and vomit.

# Praying for World Peace and Waiting To Be Sodomized in an Alley

I go to my parents' cabin for Christmas Eve. Alain is spending the holidays in Quebec City with his darling little girl. I don't feel at ease at all, alone, without Samuel to adore me and sing "Jingle Bells" with me while we do the dishes, making sure I'm doing well, and without Alain to talk for me, make my parents laugh, and let me rest my head on his lap. My protective brothers don't ask me any questions, wonder instead if I like their shirts, and compliment me on my long shiny hair. My dad thinks I'm too skinny, which makes me cry. I like my bony arms, my flat tummy and my prepubescent girl's thighs. I miss clients complimenting my physique, I'm not ready to tell my dad about the virtues of drinking two quarts of green tea and ingesting a maximum of 1,000 calories a day. My mom gets all teary-eyed every time she utters Samuel's name. Our wedding pictures still hang over the fireplace.

We go to midnight mass and can't find anywhere to sit. I tell a lady sporting a big fur coat that I'm pregnant and would like to sit down. She pushes her big Hermès handbag aside so my parents and I can sit down. My mother teases me. "It's not nice to lie in church!" I smile and tell her I'm actually one month pregnant and that my Christmas gift to her is that she'll soon be a grandmother. My parents stare at me for a moment, unable to hide their fear that Alain had already put a bun in my oven, till I kiss them on the cheek and say, "You're too funny. I'll have a long-haired Chihuahua long before I have a kid."

I play with my Anne-Marie Chagnon earrings during the sermon. I like the priest very much, and his German Shepherd who's always to his right. I feel guilty for having cheated so many times on my future ex-husband and for having saddened my parents, so I don't take part in the Eucharist. I pray for everyone's happiness, for Samuel to find a much nicer girl than me, and start using the rasor I bought him for his nose hair. I pray for Alain really to love me even when I cry in his bath tub or spend hours reading gossip magazines while he's cooking or working. I pray for my brothers to quit smoking. I want them to stay healthy. I pray for my mother to stop worrying about me and for my dad to stop being anxious even when he's not listening to Joe Dassin. I pray for world peace.

I sleep poorly after our gift exchange and the meal my mom prepared for us. I don't like sleeping alone. I crank up the heat, look at Christmas lights hanging in the trees outside and gaze at their bluish reflection in the snow. I take a pillow or two and touch myself while thinking about Alain going down on me while playing with himself, proud of his big dick and soon-to-be empty ball sack. I imagine him putting many fingers, almost his whole hand, inside me, wanting his hand to go up to the knuckles inside me, and I picture him climaxing on my belly and offering to invite other guys to join us so they'll ejaculate on me, making me all wet and sticky.

On Christmas Day, my parents drive me back to Montreal, trying in vain to convince me to join them at my grandparents', but I want to be alone and tell them spending Christmas without turkey and the whole family screaming and kissing each other won't make me sad. I want to avoid having to retell thirty times how Samuel and I broke up. I find a grocery store still open and buy some bagels, an English cucumber, and some light Philadelphia cheese spread. Alain calls me, we wish each other a merry Christmas, and he puts his daughter on who says something like Belo and drops the phone. I laugh and tell Alain I can't wait for him to get back. He tells me he put all his Vivid Entertainment porn films on his bedroom table for me.

I watch at least three episodes of the fifth season of the *Gilmore Girls* TV show while sitting in the blue Victorian armchair, applying some light pink nail polish. I drop some on the floor and panic, worried it'll stain the wooden floor, worried Alain will be mad at me forever. I watch Alain's movies, looking for one with Asian girls, and find all his films are full of gang bangs and sodomy scenes. I press rewind until I come, fantasizing on a redhead on all fours inserting a Pyrex sex toy into her best friend's snatch. I go to bed early, listen to some Satie, read Henning Mankell's *One Step Behind,* and eat two pieces of Belgian chocolate.

Samuel invites me to have brunch at the apartment on St. Denis Street with Julien and some of his colleagues from the Italian restaurant where he works. I accept his invitation and clumsily kiss him when he opens the door. I spend a good ten minutes petting each cat. I miss seeing Porcelaine run around with one of my bras in her mouth, miss laughing at Minuit sucking Syphilis' teats. Samuel tells me our rat died. "He managed to escape from his cage again, opened a garbage bag, and probably choked on a chicken bone." Sandrine's there, sticking her big boobs in everyone's face. I find her vulgar. I prepare a mango, avocado, and red pepper salad like my mom likes to make for me, and a very simple dressing. Samuel calls me "honey" by mistake. "Seeing you is like having you back for just a moment, it's doing me some good I think." He makes me uncomfortable so I have a shot of vodka. I don't say a thing about Alain, not wanting to make Samuel's friends feel awkward, but he takes me aside and says, "I keep on trying to picture your daily life with Alain, like when he comes back from work and you greet him with a smile or a kiss, or when you talk in bed after having made love, or when you cuddle with him as you fall asleep. I know I'm being masochistic but I need that pain. I don't hold a grudge, I just know I'll never be able to love somebody again. It's your fault, you left me, you quit being an escort for someone other than me. I got used to having you and your money around. What will I do now? I need to count my pennies just to buy a pack of cigarettes." I leave the apartment, furious and ashamed, asking Samuel to forgive me and wishing everyone a Happy New Year, while secretly wanting to kidnap the cats.

I go shopping on St. Denis Street and stop at Jacob where I buy a red jacket and polka dot cotton panties. I don't regret having nibbled on some snacks at the apartment while silently listening to the other guests talk. My belly's still flat. I buy extra small clothes. I also stop at Morphée where I buy a silver vase and a finely-worked wooden one I imagine full of colorful flowers, try to find a florist, and end up at Frivole buying a mini dress with a crinoline. I hop into a cab and mistakenly give the driver the wrong address. I look at the falling snow and try not to think about Samuel's accusations. I tell myself he never asked me to stop fucking other guys for money. I wonder how the new year will turn out.

Back at the condo, I spread my new clothes on the floor, remove the price tags and put them in the closet, pushing aside Alain's pants and shirts. I take a shower and shave my legs, armpits, and pussy, making sure to open my lips so I won't forget a single hair. I choose to wear my new Jacob panties even though I haven't washed them yet. I smooth my hair with a straightening iron, choosing the same products I used when I worked at the escort agency, golden Nuxe lotion on my breasts, shoulder blades, and legs, St. Ives skin firming lotion on my ass and belly, and drops of Givenchy's Very Irresistible perfume inside my elbows and knees.

I wait for Alain's return while reading an article about celebrities who had botched plastic surgeries, and he tells me I'm beautiful, saying I should dress like that to celebrate the New Year in a few days at Sofa with his friends. I force him to undress. He pushes me against the wall, admitting, "I've only jerked myself off once, while taking a shower, a finger in my ass. I'll fill your mouth to the brim." He wakes me during the night and, wanting to sleep, I tell him no, I'm warm under the covers, and I don't want to move. He's hurt and offended. He doesn't understand that I'm refusing because I'm tired. He thinks I don't want him. In order to ease his paranoia, I take his dick and direct it towards my cunt. He grunts, biting my shoulders, and gently climaxes between my thighs.

I sign up for art history classes. During my last free days before the start of the semester in mid-January, I spend most of my days at the downtown bookstore Chapters by the Cours Mont-Royal mall. I buy English-language books for teenage girls, and fashion and design magazines, and read them at a table by a large window at Café République. Today, I get up at noon. Alain's already gone to work and left me a little note on the counter. Though I can hardly make out his illegible script, it makes me happy. I go to the Belgo gallery where I once blew a friend in the old elevator and notice a mirror hung on a bare white wall.

On it, there's an engraving, "You are still here." It immediately strikes a chord, sowing confusion in me. I feel dizzy and can't help but stare at the piece, looking at my own face and those words carved in the glass. I think about the agency, about my thousands of clients, about all those times when I feared getting seriously sick. I think about that time when I burned my skin with wax, about my pussy that was so often sore but always wet, about my body which never let me down, about my body that's tough despite only weighing ninety-five pounds, about Samuel who let me risk it all, our relationship and my life. I think about Alain and how I love him as an adult, and not as a kid who believes all the promises made to her will come true. I love Alain who sometimes drinks too much and gets mad at the whole world, telling me about his favorite punk bands, communism, and the filmmaker Wim Wenders. He doesn't like my tears or the smell of my self-tanning lotion, but wants to have kids with me, kids that would run around, getting their Gap and Tommy Hilfiger Child clothes dirty, kids that would steal my necklaces and try on my high stiletto shoes. "You are still here." Even though my parents would have wanted me to take longer to decide to move into the St. Henri neighborhood. "You are still here." Even though I sometimes think I have no future when Alain's mad and says he wants to be alone, again, or leave the country and settle in Kenya, or go back to France. There is no future without him. I want to stay there and not answer Debbie's calls asking me to come back to the agency. I only want someone who has time to make love to me slowly and who doesn't think I'm ridiculous drinking raspberry-flavored vodka in front of the American reality TV show *Big Brother*.

I leave the Belgo shaken and walk to Café République, my head in the clouds, not noticing the cold, forgetting that I have gloves in my black Guess purse. I order a Brie and honey sandwich, telling myself that if Alain doesn't want me anymore, I could buy myself some big boobs and collagen lip injections and become an even more sought-after escort, more porn star than girl-next-door, and more mechanical than loving. It's not every day that I believe in Alain's love. I sometimes wonder if it was all a game, if he needed me to fall for him, had to prove to himself that he's attractive and deserved all he wanted even though his wife left him on his birthday. I leaf through an *InStyle* without caring about the bread crumbs falling on the pages, on my burgundy wool sweater, on my American Apparel leggings. I can't wait for the summer, to get tanned on the balcony, wearing a Marciano bikini, with a Candace Bushnell novel in my hands, to walk to the Atwater Market to have a *pain au chocolat* or an almond croissant every morning and buy some cape gooseberries, plums, or beets with my mom, and to run on the bike path until I collapse on the grass when my feet or lungs hurt from having run too fast. I can't wait to walk around in really short dresses and ask Alain to fuck me in an alley, to call me a slut in front of the neighbors, and to show me how to bake a *gratin dauphinois* without burning it. I can't wait to believe this is real and that I'll never go back to a basement apartment, crying in front of the dirty dishes for wanting of a better life.

# Kinky and Pretty Without Needing To Hear It from Two Hundred Guys a Month

I've tried to finish my literature and art history degree for the past year. I've also tried to be happy doing yoga and aerobics in front of reality TV shows, and believing I was pretty without thirty or so clients telling me each week. I couldn't. I'd go out with Alain, drink too much, smile at the barmaids he used to fuck, always thinking they were prettier than me. Every day I hopped on a scale, and spent all my savings on sexy dresses, and died a little each time an extra small dress wouldn't fit me well because of my small breasts.

When I was an escort I thought I was amazing. My clients kept telling me not to change, they paid to have sex with me when hundreds of other girls in Montreal were also offering their bodies. Alone, being only Alain's, having to be faithful to him, not calling back clients who missed me, was hard. I didn't feel as womanly as before. I still knew how to whore myself out. I shaved every day and woke up in the middle of the night my mouth full with Alain's dick. I knew how to smile but didn't know what else to do. I didn't know how to see myself as anything other than a former escort. Suddenly, I was nothing. I hated myself each time I realized I missed the agency. I was addicted to having lots of bills in my envelopes, addicted to all those dicks that came inside of me. I still remembered my sore cunt and how my hair became dull and flat after a couple of hours' work, but I didn't care about that anymore. I was telling myself that I would be ready to start again.

I wondered if Alain saw me as nothing but a former escort, if his desire to have kids with me was fed only by his sadness of not having his little girl around all the time, if he wouldn't one day find me too dumb for him because I know nothing about African history and can't cook anything but mocha-flavored cupcakes. I wasn't happy with him for a long time, feeling stupid and ridiculous for thinking it's possible to be loved after being paid for sex. For his part, he worried about his age and my desire for other men. He couldn't believe a girl who had sex with two hundred men a month could be satisfied being with just one.

During that time I decided to get breast implants. To feel more like a woman and reject that little girl image clients loved so much. I followed my surgeon's advice and gained some weight so the operation wouldn't be too risky. I happily ate a slice of pizza for lunch every day for a month. I spent a day at the Fleury Hospital, where a nurse asked me, not without a touch of envy, how much a breast augmentation surgery cost. I read a *Cosmopolitan* magazine before the anesthesia and left the hospital with a bandage going all the way up to the base of my neck, my back and sides in a lot of pain, craving a chocolate milkshake and wanting to fall asleep on the grass in front of the condo. I was too hot under my Juicy Couture sweatshirt and had to walk bent over double, afraid I'd never be able to walk erect again because of my new very heavy boobs filled with saline water. I wondered if I'd have to spend the rest of my life staring at the cracks in the sidewalk, my eyes fixed on my ugly feet stuck in tight but pretty shoes, yellow patent leather like those worn by a *Harper's Bazaar* model in a summer issue. Alain thought I was fat. He liked my new boobs, but not being able to touch them, bite them, or push them against a window as he used to annoyed him. He didn't want to have to wait for my tits to get less sore. At night, I touched my breasts, sticking my nails in my skin to feel the demarcation of the implants. Thinking of my new bra size made me happy. I went from 32A to 34C, from schoolgirl to wannabe Victoria Beckham.

I also chose to dye my hair blonde and Alain was very scared of how other men might look at me, thinking I could leave him at any moment for no other reason than having big boobs and Marilyn Monroe's hairdo. He used to say I wasn't good at loving him, and I told him he didn't have to love me at all.

After a year running through my savings, buying almond croissants at the Atwater Market bakery and dresses I wore only once when going out with Alain and his friends, I decided to look for work. I looked through the same papers I had leafed through to find an escort agency and answered the wanted ads. I finally found work in a jewelry store where I was surrounded by women. My colleagues as well as all the clients were women, and I found it surreal and hard to bond with them for $10 an hour. I was bored and kept thinking about how much I could make for a condom-less blow job and what I could buy at the jewelry store if I was still an escort.

I quit that job after a few months and became a downtown Montreal librarian once more as well as a webcam hostess in the most famous studio in the province. I had fun walking from the library with my Lululemon gym bag full of sex toys to the studio where I became, after only four months, the most popular girl on the Website. I was super proud of myself but had to quit because Alain couldn't handle the thought of his girlfriend spending her days topless, on all fours, trying to virtually seduce other men. I understood.

But my sexuality was still very important to me and I needed to share it with others. That's how I came to writing.

I don't know what would have become of me had I not been an escort. I probably would have had a constant doctor's prescription for Xanax in my purse, spent my days playing with myself, dissatisfied with my life, crying all the time, envying my neighbors with big tits as much as Hollywood stars clutching Louis Vuitton handbags. My incursion into the sex industry allowed me to know myself better and accept myself as an almost permanently wet girl who likes to dance while listening to Britney Spears songs. I no longer feel like a phony, or ignore my desires, or deny my superficiality, and ceased wanting to caress my wrists with a razor blade.

I'm not unique. There are hundreds of girls like me who are escorts, strippers, webcam hostesses, or porn stars who have never been raped, don't do drugs, don't have any sexually transmitted infections, and have fun spreading their legs without any guilt or regrets except being rejected by a society that stigmatizes them and prefers to see them as victims.

I am not a victim. I chose to become an escort to do exactly what I dreamed of doing.

And I continue to believe all is possible, that by choosing to work in the sex industry women can learn to assert themselves, make the most of their bodies, their youth, and the easy pleasures of the flesh.

I'll never forget that if "girls just wanna have fun," men do also, and I'll always strive not to be like the wives my clients used to criticize. I lick my boyfriend's balls, shave my pussy, and thank God for having given me miles and miles of dicks so I'll be more respectful of what I am and what men are. I know they're not all perverts or liars even though they see escorts.

I see them the way I see myself. They only want happiness,

and good for them if it lasts more than an hour and costs less than $200. There's nothing wrong with seeing a whore or buying yourself a vibrator or tons of Chupa Chups lollipops if that makes your life better and puts a smile on your face.

www.melodienelson.com

www.transitpublishing.com